TABLE DES MATIÈRES

TEN PROFITABLE JOBS YOU CAN DO WITHOUT SKILLS, THANKS TO AI

Earn Money Easily with Artificial Intelligence

KOUADIO KONAN JOEL

Cover Designer: Painter
Library of Congress Control Number: 2018675309
Printed in the United States of America

TEN PROFITABLE JOBS TO DO WITHOUT SKILLS THANKS TO AI

Earn Money Easily with Artificial Intelligence

PREFACE

The digital age we live in is marked by unprecedented technological developments. One of the most fascinating and transformative revolutions of recent years is the emergence of artificial intelligence (AI). This technology, which seemed like the preserve of science fiction, is now within reach and is gradually becoming part of our daily lives. Moreover, it is redefining the professions, roles, and skills required for success in the professional world.

This book, The 10 Jobs You Can Do Without Skills Thanks to AI , explores how it's now possible to launch a career and thrive in various fields without having any specific prior skills. Yes, you read that right: you can start a business, generate income, and build a thriving business, even if you don't have any specialized skills.

AI plays a vital role in this transformation by empowering anyone with powerful, intuitive, and accessible tools. Traditional jobs, often requiring long-standing expertise, can now be addressed through AI-powered platforms, software, and tools that automate processes and assist users at every stage of their business.

In this book, we'll explore a variety of careers where artificial intelligence is becoming a strategic ally. From virtual assistance to customer relationship management, content creation, and digital marketing, these fields are now accessible to everyone. You don't need a computer science degree or years of professional experience to get started. AI fills this gap by simplifying and automating complex tasks.

This book isn't just a list of opportunities. It's an invitation to rethink the way you work, embrace the technological tools shaping tomorrow's world, and create new revenue streams without the burden of traditional specialized skills. If you've always dreamed of starting a business or changing career path but felt limited by your lack of training, this book shows you how AI can be the key to overcoming this obstacle.

Throughout the pages, you'll discover concrete strategies, practical tools, and advice to help you get started in these innovative professions right away. Whether you're changing careers, a student, or simply looking for new opportunities, this book will help you understand how AI can help you create and manage a profitable business, without the need for advanced technical skills.

AI doesn't replace humans, but it does open new doors. By mastering it, you'll have the opportunity to position yourself in booming sectors and participate in the digital workplace with confidence.

Welcome to a future where possibilities are endless.

INTRODUCTION

Artificial intelligence (AI) is revolutionizing the world of work, automating tasks once reserved for experts. Thanks to technological advances, many jobs can now be performed without advanced technical skills. This book explores 10 careers accessible to everyone thanks to AI , detailing the tools available and the steps to get started.

The evolution of AI and its impact on the world of work

AI has grown at a rapid pace in recent years. Once the preserve of research labs and large corporations, it's now integrated into tools accessible to the general public. ChatGPT, Midjourney, Synthesia, DALL·E, and many others allow anyone to produce content, manage an online business, or even automate complex tasks without prior training.

Some major transformations in the labor market thanks to AI:

Automation of repetitive tasks : Many administrative and customer service jobs are increasingly being taken over by AI.

Democratization of skills : AI makes accessible professions that previously required years of learning, such as writing, design or video creation.

New emerging professions : the rise of AI

technologies has given rise to new professional opportunities, particularly in freelancing and digital entrepreneurship.

Today, AI is no longer just a tool, but a real lever of opportunities for those who know how to use it intelligently.

Why does AI allow us to perform jobs without advanced skills?

Contrary to popular belief, artificial intelligence does not completely replace humans, but it automates and simplifies complex tasks . Thus, people without technical expertise can now:

Create content (texts, images, videos, training) without knowing how to write, draw or edit videos .

Manage online businesses without management or programming knowledge .

Develop services and automate processes to generate passive income .

AI functions as a high-performance assistant that completes tasks in minutes instead of hours or days. You just need to learn how to use the right tools to take advantage of it.

How to use this book to get started?

This book is designed as a practical guide to help you get started without any specific skills or prior experience .

Here's how to approach it effectively:

1.Browse the 10 careers on offer and identify the one that appeals to you the most.

2.Read each part to understand how AI can help you in this profession.

3.Follow the practical steps and discover recommended AI tools to get started right away.

4.Apply what you learn by testing the tools and launching your business.

This book will give you the keys to quickly and effectively getting started in a career facilitated by AI. It's your turn!

PART 1: CREATOR OF EBOOKS AND SELF-PUBLISHED BOOKS

Chapter 1: Understanding Self-Publishing With Ai

1. The rise of ebooks and self-publishing

Self-publishing has exploded in recent years, thanks to the rise of digital technology and universally accessible platforms. Today, anyone can publish a book without going through a traditional publishing house. Platforms like Amazon Kindle Direct Publishing (KDP), Kobo Writing Life and Apple Books allow you to sell ebooks to a wide audience, without any initial investment.

This phenomenon can be explained by several factors:

•The democratization of digital technology : More and more readers prefer ebooks to physical books for their practicality and lower cost.

•Low barriers to entry : Unlike traditional publishing, self-publishing does not require publisher approval, giving authors complete freedom.

•A growing market : With millions of readers worldwide, it is possible to generate passive income by publishing one or more well-targeted ebooks.

However, one of the biggest barriers to self-publishing is the writing process itself. Many people want to write a book, but don't know where to start or think they lack the necessary skills. This is where artificial intelligence comes in.

2. Why AI makes writing easier

Artificial intelligence has revolutionized writing by allowing anyone to create an ebook quickly and efficiently. Thanks to tools like ChatGPT, Jasper AI, or Claude AI , it is now possible to:

•Generate ideas and structure an outline : AI can suggest popular topics, organize chapters, and structure a book in minutes.

•Write content quickly : No need to spend months writing! AI can generate entire paragraphs based on your topic and style.

•Improve text quality : Tools like Grammarly or ProWritingAid can help improve grammar, style, and text flow.

•Create compelling descriptions and summaries : AI can write compelling descriptions to attract readers to sales platforms.

With these tools, even someone with no writing skills can publish a professional book in record time. The key is knowing how to use AI effectively to create quality content that will provide value to readers.

3. Platforms for selling your ebooks

Once your book is written, it's time to put it up for sale. Several platforms allow you to publish and sell ebooks with no upfront costs:

·Amazon Kindle Direct Publishing (KDP) : The most popular platform for publishing books in digital and paper versions, with a large international audience.

·Kobo Writing Life : Ideal for reaching readers using Kobo e-readers and for reaching a French-speaking audience.

·Apple Books : Allows you to sell ebooks on the App Store and reach Apple users.

·Google Play Books : Provides visibility to readers using Android and Google Books.

·Gumroad & Payhip : Platforms that allow you to sell ebooks directly and receive 100% of the revenue without going through an intermediary.

·Shopify or WooCommerce : For those who want to sell directly on their own site and maintain complete control over sales and pricing.

The choice of platform depends on your goals. To maximize your sales, it is recommended to publish on multiple platforms at once.

With the help of artificial intelligence, self-publishing is becoming an accessible and profitable way to generate passive income. In the next chapters, we'll see how to effectively use AI to successfully write, format, and promote your ebook.

Chapter 2: Writing An Ebook With Chatgpt

1. Generate ideas and structure a book

One of the most important steps in writing an ebook is generating ideas and structuring the content . Thanks to artificial intelligence, it is now possible to simplify this task and quickly obtain relevant and well-organized ideas.

Why use ChatGPT for this step?

·AI can analyze market trends and suggest popular topics.

·It helps to structure a detailed plan based on your niche and target audience.

·It offers eye-catching headlines and powerful summaries to captivate readers from the start.

How to generate ideas with ChatGPT?

1.Ask the right questions : Ask the AI to suggest topics related to your area of interest. For example:

"What are the most popular ebook topics in 2024?"

"What are the common problems people are looking to solve?"

2.Select a profitable niche : ChatGPT can help you identify under-tapped markets where competition is low but demand is high.

3.Create a detailed outline : Once you've chosen your topic, ask the AI to structure the book. For example:

"Can you give me a detailed outline for an ebook on [chosen topic]?"

Example of a plan generated by ChatGPT for an ebook on personal development:

1.Introduction

2.Chapter 1: Understanding the Basics of Personal Development

Definition and fundamental principles

The benefits of a conscious approach

How to start your development journey

3.Chapter 2: Building an Effective Routine

The Importance of Habits

Examples of effective routines

Monitoring and adjustment

4.Conclusion and next steps

With this method, it becomes easy to structure a book in a logical and engaging way.

2. Write effectively with AI

Once the structure is defined, it's time to move on to writing. ChatGPT allows you to write content smoothly and quickly, without requiring advanced writing skills.

Techniques for writing an ebook with ChatGPT

1.Write a first draft quickly

You can ask the AI to write an entire chapter by giving it a structure.

Sample assignment:

"Can you write a chapter on 'The Basics of Minimalism' in three sections: introduction, benefits, and how to get started?"

ChatGPT then generates a text that you can modify and improve.

2.Adapt the tone and style

If you want a more formal or engaging tone, let the AI know.

Example: "Write this chapter with an inspiring and motivating tone."

3.Add examples and anecdotes

To make your text more engaging, ask ChatGPT to add stories or case studies.

Example: "Add a concrete example of someone who has succeeded using this method."

4.Divide the text into clear sections

ChatGPT can structure chapters with subheadings, bullet points, and summaries to make the text more readable.

By following these techniques, you can write a complete ebook in just a few days, instead of months.

3. Verification and correction with AI

While ChatGPT is a powerful tool, it's important to proofread and improve your content before publishing. Fortunately, there are several AI tools that can help you refine your content.

The steps of proofreading and correction with AI:

1.Grammar and spelling correction

Use Grammarly, Antidote, or LanguageTool to detect and correct spelling and grammar mistakes.

2.Improved style and clarity

ChatGPT can rephrase sentences to make them sound more fluid and natural.

Command: "Can you reword this paragraph to make it clearer and more concise?"

3.Checking consistency and structure

Make sure the ideas flow logically and that each chapter adds value.

You can ask ChatGPT: "Can you analyze this text and tell me if it is coherent and well-structured?"

4.Plagiarism detection

To avoid any duplication issues, use a tool like Copyscape or Quetext to check the originality of your content.

Once these steps are complete, your ebook will be ready for formatting and publishing. In the next chapter, we'll cover how to format and prepare your ebook for professional distribution.

Chapter 3: Automated Layout And Design

1. Using Canva and Atticus

Once your ebook is written and proofread, careful layout is essential to ensure a pleasant and professional read. Fortunately, AI and automated tools make this step much easier.

Why is layout important?

•Improves the reading experience : Well-structured and well-spaced text is more engaging.

•Builds Credibility : A professional ebook attracts more readers and sales.

•Facilitates acceptance on platforms : Amazon KDP, Apple Books or Kobo require a correct format.

Canva: a simple and effective tool

Canva is a great tool for formatting your ebook, especially if you're just starting out. It allows you to create:

•Elegant layouts with pre-designed templates.

•Well-structured chapters with highlighted headings and subheadings.

•Illustrations and icons to make reading more attractive.

How to use Canva for layout?

1.Choose an ebook template : Canva offers free and

paid templates.

2.Add your text : Copy and paste each chapter and adjust the font, size, and spacing.

3.Insert images and illustrations : Canva's AI can generate relevant visuals.

4.Export to PDF or EPUB : These formats are accepted by most self-publishing platforms.

Atticus: An all-in-one solution for authors

Atticus is a more advanced alternative that allows you to:

•Automatically format an ebook effortlessly.

•Create EPUB and MOBI versions suitable for e-readers .

•Generate a dynamic table of contents .

How to use Atticus?

1.Import your text directly into the tool.

2.Customize the layout by choosing a professional book style.

3.Export the final file ready for publishing to Amazon KDP or other platforms.

 Tip : Canva is great for custom design, while Atticus is perfect for ebook-optimized layouts.

2. Creating covers with AI

The cover is the key element that attracts readers. A poorly designed cover can reduce your sales , even if your content is excellent. Thanks to AI, it's now easy to create attractive covers without design skills .

AI tools for creating covers

1.Canva AI : Offers templates and automatically generates designs.

2.BookBrush : Specializes in creating book covers.

3.Midjourney / DALL·E : Generates unique images with AI.

How to create a cover with AI?

1.Determine the style : Minimalist, futuristic, realistic...

2.Use an AI image generator to design a unique illustration.

3.Add the title and subtitle on Canva or BookBrush .

4.Optimize the resolution : A good cover should be 300 dpi and respect the dimensions of the chosen platform.

 Tip : Test several versions and ask your audience for feedback before choosing the final cover.

3. Prepare a file ready to publish

Once the layout and cover are complete, the book needs to be converted into a format compatible with self-publishing platforms.

Most used ebook formats

•PDF : Ideal for selling on your own website.

•EPUB : Standard format for Kindle, Apple Books and

Kobo.

•MOBI : Old Kindle format (Amazon now accepts EPUB).

Tools for converting your ebook

1.Calibre : Easily convert a Word document to EPUB or MOBI.

2.Atticus : Automatically handles EPUB and PDF formats.

3.Kindle Create : Amazon's official tool for formatting your ebook.

Pre-publication checklist

✓ Final Proofreading : Check the content for consistency.

✓ Test on different e-readers : Use the Amazon KDP preview.

✓ Adding metadata : Author name, description, keywords.

✓ File validation : Make sure it meets platform standards.

Once these steps are completed, your ebook is ready to be published and sold! ☐ In the next chapter, we will see how to publish and promote your ebook to generate passive income.

Chapter 4: Publishing And Selling Your Book

1. Amazon KDP and other platforms

Once your ebook is ready, you need to publish it on the right platforms to maximize your visibility and sales.

Why choose Amazon KDP?

Amazon Kindle Direct Publishing (KDP) is the most popular self-publishing platform for several reasons:

• Access to a wide audience : Amazon represents more than 80% of the ebook market.

• Attractive royalties : Up to 70% commission on each sale.

• Fast publishing : Your ebook can be available in less than 24 hours .

How to publish on Amazon KDP?

1.Create an account at kdp.amazon.com .

2.Add a new book and fill in the information (title, description, keywords).

3.Upload your file (EPUB or PDF format).

4.Set a price and choose the royalty option (35% or 70%).

5.Start publishing and wait for Amazon's approval (usually within 24 hours).

Other popular platforms

•Apple Books : Widely used on iPhone and iPad.

•Kobo Writing Life : Particularly popular in Europe and Canada.

·Google Play Books : Ideal for reaching Android users.

·Gumroad & Payhip : Perfect for selling directly to readers with greater control over pricing.

✓ Tip : Posting on multiple platforms helps increase your reach and sales.

2. AI Marketing Strategies to Boost Sales

A good marketing strategy is essential to getting your ebook noticed and generating sales. With AI, you can automate and optimize several aspects of marketing.

Create a catchy description with AI

AI can help you write a compelling description that attracts readers:

·Use ChatGPT to generate a persuasive description by incorporating keywords.

·Test several versions and choose the one that converts best.

Amazon Advertising (AMS) powered by AI

Amazon Ads is a great way to promote your ebook. You can use:

·Helium 10 's AI to analyze profitable keywords.

·ChatGPT for writing impactful ads.

Automated email marketing

·Use tools like Mailchimp or ConvertKit to send promotional emails.

·Segment your audience to better target interested

readers.

•Automate follow-ups to maximize sales.

Social Media and AI Content

•Post excerpts from your book on Instagram, Facebook, and TikTok with AI (e.g., Canva).

•Automate your posts with tools like Buffer and Hootsuite .

•Use ChatGPT to create engaging posts.

✓ Tip : Use strategic hashtags (#ebook, #selfpublishing , #Kindle) to reach more people.

3. Advanced ebook monetization

Once your ebook is published, there are several strategies to maximize your earnings.

1. Sell bundles (packages)

•Offer multiple ebooks at a discounted price to increase perceived value .

•Example: A pack of 3 books on productivity sold for €20, instead of €10 each.

2. Create a subscription or community

•Use Patreon or Substack to offer exclusive content to readers.

•Example: Book summaries, personalized advice...

3. Offer additional services

•Offer personalized coaching based on the content of your book.

•Example: If you write about productivity, offer coaching sessions.

4. Sell alternative formats

•✓ Audiobook : Use AI tools like Speechify or Murf AI to create an audiobook .

•✓ Paperback : Publish on demand with KDP Print .

✓ Tip : The more formats and options you offer, the more you multiply your revenue streams.

Chapter Summary

✓ Amazon KDP is the best platform for publishing your ebook , but other options exist.

✓ AI helps automate promotion and marketing to maximize sales.

✓ Advanced strategies like subscriptions and add-on services can significantly increase revenue.

PART 2: AI-ASSISTED CONTENT WRITER

Chapter 1: The Importance Of Online Content

1.1. Why is content essential on the Internet?

Content is the backbone of the web . Every page we visit, every ad we see, and every social media post relies on written content. Understanding its role and impact helps us maximize the opportunities of AI-powered writing .

✓The role of content in SEO and visibility

Natural search engine optimization (SEO) is based on the quality and relevance of content . Google prioritizes pages that provide informative value and respond to user queries.

•Good, well-structured content with optimized keywords improves Google rankings.

•Long, detailed articles are more likely to be shared and receive backlinks .

•A site with an active blog attracts up to 55% more traffic than a site without regular content.

Example: An e-commerce site that publishes SEO-optimized buying guides sees its pages rank higher and attracts more visitors.

✓ The impact of quality articles on sales and engagement

Content not only serves to inform, it also influences purchasing decisions :

•Good storytelling around a product increases its appeal.

•Educational blog articles reassure customers before purchasing.

•Good copywriting improves the conversion rate on a sales page.

Example: An online store selling dietary supplements can attract more customers with a blog about the benefits of nutrition.

✓ Examples of sites that succeed thanks to content

1.HubSpot – Marketing blog that generates millions of visitors and sells software through its content.

2.Neil Patel – SEO expert who drives traffic with in-depth articles and sells his consulting services.

3.Shopify Blog – E-commerce guide that boosts sales by helping entrepreneurs.

✓ Key takeaway : A well-thought-out content strategy can help you attract free traffic and effectively monetize your site.

1.2. The different types of written content

Each online platform has its own content

requirements , so it's essential to adapt to audience formats and expectations.

✓ Blog posts and SEO

·Allows you to attract regular traffic via Google.

·Can be optimized with ChatGPT to speed up writing.

·Effective Strategy: Detailed Guides, Lists, and Case Studies .

Example: A fitness blog that publishes a detailed guide on "How to Lose Weight in 30 Days" can generate traffic for years.

✓ Newsletters and marketing emails

·One of the most cost-effective tools in digital marketing.

·Allows you to create a direct relationship with your audience.

·Tools like ChatGPT help automate the creation of engaging newsletters.

Example: A personal development coach sends a weekly newsletter with tips and exclusive offers to build audience loyalty.

✓ Content for social networks

·impactful posts (Instagram, Facebook, Twitter).

·Engaging content like carousels and Twitter threads .

·AI helps quickly generate captions and post ideas .

Example: A community manager uses ChatGPT and Canva to create and schedule 30 posts in a single day.

✓ Takeaway : Each type of content has its benefits and can be automated with AI to save time.

1.3. Opportunities for content writers

The demand for written content is exploding with the rise of digital technology. Numerous opportunities are opening up for writers, especially by integrating AI tools to maximize their productivity.

✓ Freelancing (writing for clients)

•Platforms like Upwork , Fiverr , Textbroker to find missions.

•Clients are looking for writers who can produce SEO-optimized content .

•With AI, a writer can produce more content in less time and increase their revenue.

Example: A writer charges €100 for a 1000-word article, which he writes in 30 minutes with ChatGPT instead of 2 hours.

✓ Creating a monetized blog

•Generate income with Google AdSense , affiliate marketing and selling digital products .

•AI helps write articles quickly and optimize SEO.

•A well-positioned blog can become a source of passive income .

Example: A travel blog monetized through Amazon Affiliates earns several hundred euros per month.

Using AI to produce content faster

•ChatGPT, Jasper AI and Copy.ai allow you to write 5 to 10 times faster .

•AI tools to generate ideas, reformulate and correct texts .

•Ideal for freelancers and entrepreneurs who want to optimize their time.

Example: A freelance writer uses ChatGPT to generate an article outline , then adapts it with their expertise to deliver quality content.

Chapter Summary

✓ Content is essential for online visibility and sales.

✓ Different types of content exist: blogs, emails, social networks .

✓ Many opportunities exist to monetize writing , especially with AI .

Chapter 2: Using Chatgpt And Other Ai Tools

Artificial Intelligence is revolutionizing online content writing. With tools like ChatGPT , content creators, bloggers, and entrepreneurs can produce articles, posts, and emails in minutes . However, to get the most out of these tools, it's essential to know how to use them properly, optimize the generated content, and avoid common mistakes .

2.1. ChatGPT: A powerful assistant for writing

ChatGPT is one of the most advanced tools for AI-assisted writing . It allows you to quickly generate content, rephrase sentences, and improve the flow of texts .

How to generate an article in a few minutes?

1.Define the subject and objective

Example: "Write an article on the benefits of minimalism."

Determine the target audience and desired writing style .

2.Use specific prompts

"Can you write a 1000-word article on minimalism with an introduction, three sections, and a conclusion?"

"Can you add concrete examples and statistics to support the arguments?"

3.Optimize the structure and refine the content

Check for consistency and add smooth transitions .

Complete with relevant sources and citations .

✓ Optimize text quality with effective prompts

A good prompt improves the quality of the generated text. Here are some examples:

•For a structured article:

"Write a 1,500-word article on stock market investing.

Structure it with an introduction, three detailed sections, and a conclusion."

•To improve an existing text:

"Rewrite this paragraph to make it more impactful and fluid."

•For a specific tone:

"Can you write this text with an inspiring and motivating tone? "

✓ Correct and reformulate with AI

•Stylistic improvement : "Make this text more fluid and natural."

•Reducing repetition : "Simplify this sentence without losing its meaning."

•Grammar correction : "Correct the mistakes and improve the syntax of this text."

✓ Takeaway : ChatGPT is a great starting point, but you should always proofread and refine the generated content.

2.2. Other AI tools to improve writing

In addition to ChatGPT, several tools allow you to refine writing, optimize SEO and improve text quality .

✓ Grammarly and QuillBot for proofreading and styling

•Grammarly : Corrects spelling mistakes and suggests stylistic improvements.

•QuillBot : Allows you to reformulate a text in several styles (formal, creative, concise).

✓ Example use case : An article generated by ChatGPT can be proofread and improved with Grammarly to avoid errors and optimize readability.

✓ SurferSEO and Frase.io for SEO

•SurferSEO : Analyzes keywords and compares text to top-ranked articles on Google.

•Frase.io : Helps structure an article to match Internet users' search intentions.

✓ Example of use : Before publishing an article, use SurferSEO to adjust the number of keywords and improve natural referencing.

Jasper AI and Writesonic for Optimized Content Creation

•Jasper AI : Generates texts optimized for digital marketing and SEO.

•Writesonic : Quickly create product descriptions, advertisements, and blog content.

✓ Example use case : An e-commerce entrepreneur can generate Amazon-optimized product descriptions in seconds with Jasper AI.

✓ Key takeaway : Combining multiple tools helps optimize content and produce professional-quality text .

2.3. *Avoid mistakes and maintain a human style*

One of the risks of writing with AI is producing text that's too generic, robotic, or soulless . Here's how to avoid these pitfalls and make your content more authentic.

✓ How to avoid text that is too robotic?

•Do not publish raw AI-generated text without modification.

•Add anecdotes, personal opinions and concrete examples .

•Check that the tone matches the target audience .

Example: A blog post about personal development will be more engaging if it includes personal experiences and practical advice rather than just an AI-generated list of tips.

 The importance of personalizing and adding your personal touch

•Rewrite some parts by adding your expertise.

•Use specific keywords that are tailored to your audience.

•Insert quotes or references to make the content credible.

Example: A writer can improve an AI-generated article by adding real testimonials or case studies to make it more authentic.

✓ Verify and validate information generated by AI

•Always cross-reference sources and check the reliability of the data.

•Avoid misinformation or approximations generated by AI.

•Proofread carefully to ensure the text is consistent and logical .

✓ Key takeaway : AI is a great assistant , but it's the human who adds value by personalizing the content.

Chapter Summary

✓ ChatGPT helps you quickly write articles and optimize content.

✓ Tools like Grammarly, SurferSEO , and Jasper AI help improve quality and SEO.

✓ To avoid overly robotic content, personalize, reword, and verify information .

Chapter 3: Monetizing Your Articles (Blog, Freelance, Etc.)

Written content isn't just about informing or entertaining—it can also generate significant income . Whether it's freelancing, creating a profitable blog, or selling content in various forms , there are several strategies for monetizing your writing skills. This chapter explores the best methods for turning writing into a sustainable source of income.

3.1. Becoming a freelance writer

Freelancing is one of the fastest and most affordable ways to monetize your writing skills. Many clients seek writers to create articles, product descriptions, marketing emails, or social media content.

✓ Platforms for finding clients

To get started as a freelance writer, you can register on several platforms that connect freelancers and businesses:

•Fiverr : Ideal for offering services at attractive prices and gaining visibility.

•Upwork : International platform that allows you to land well-paid contracts.

•Malt : Very popular in France, ideal for collaborating with local businesses.

✓ Tip : It's important to create an attractive profile , post work samples, and accumulate positive reviews to get more clients.

Strategies to stand out and set your prices

•Specialization : Choose a profitable niche (SEO, finance, tech, health, etc.).

•Portfolio : Create a personal website or blog to showcase your skills.

•Pricing : Don't undervalue your work. Charge based on the value you provide, not just the number of words.

✓ Example of prices :

•Beginner: €0.05 to €0.08 per word

·Intermediate: €0.10 to €0.15 per word

·Expert: €0.20 to €0.50 per word and more

✓ How AI can speed up work and increase revenue

AI can help with:

✓ Drafting faster with ChatGPT .

✓ Improving SEO with SurferSEO and Frase.io .

✓ Editing and rewording with Grammarly and QuillBot .

✓ Tip : A writer who uses AI effectively can produce 2-3 times more articles in a single time , thus increasing their income.

3.2. Create and monetize a blog

A well-built blog can become a source of passive income through various monetization strategies.

✓ Find a profitable niche and attract traffic

A profitable niche must meet the following criteria:

·High demand (example: finance, entrepreneurship, wellness).

·SEO potential (lots of Google searches on the topic).

·Possibility of monetization (affiliation, training, digital products).

✓ Useful tools : Google Trends, Ubersuggest , Ahrefs to analyze trends.

✓ Monetization through advertising, affiliation and training

1.Advertisement :

Google AdSense : Generates passive income by displaying ads.

Premium ad networks: Mediavine , Ezoic (for blogs with high traffic).

2.Affiliation :

Amazon Associates: Commission on each product sold through a link.

Direct partnerships: Promote software or training.

3.Sale of training courses and ebooks :

Convert articles into paid PDF guides .

Create online courses via Teachable , Podia or Gumroad .

✓ Example of a profitable blog : An investment blog can generate income through sponsored articles, affiliate marketing on trading platforms, and the sale of stock market training courses .

Automate publishing with AI

AI can help plan content in advance :

✓ Write articles with ChatGPT and Jasper AI .

✓ Generate visuals with Canva and Midjourney .

✓ Schedule posts with WordPress and tools like Buffer .

3.3. Selling content in different forms

Beyond articles and blogs, it is possible to monetize

your content in various forms .

✓ Offer paid guides and ebooks

A well-structured ebook can be sold on Amazon KDP, Gumroad, or Payhip .

✓ Idea : Turn your best articles into a premium PDF guide and sell it through a blog or newsletter.

✓ Write scripts for YouTube videos

Many YouTubers pay writers to write engaging scripts .

✓ Platforms to offer this service : Fiverr , Upwork , or contact creators directly on YouTube .

✓ Create a monetized newsletter

A newsletter can generate revenue through:

✓ Paid subscriptions (via Substack , Ghost).

✓ Sponsorships and product placements.

✓ Promoting services and personal training.

✓ Example : A newsletter about entrepreneurship can be monetized with ads and exclusive training .

Chapter Summary

✓ Freelancing is a great option to immediately monetize your writing skills.

✓ A well-optimized blog can become a source of passive income through advertising, affiliate marketing, and training sales.

✓ It is possible to sell content in different forms , such

as ebooks, scripts or monetized newsletters.

Chapter 4: Optimizing Your Ai Writing Activity

With the advancement of artificial intelligence, writers can become more productive, improve the quality of their content, and diversify their revenue streams . This chapter explores strategies to maximize efficiency, build audience loyalty, and move toward more profitable opportunities.

4.1. Save time and produce efficiently

The intelligent use of AI allows you to optimize your workflow and increase your production without sacrificing quality .

Automate topic research and idea generation

Finding relevant and trending topics is essential to attract attention and improve your SEO.

Useful tools :

•Google Trends : Identify popular topics.

•AnswerThePublic : Find frequently asked questions from internet users.

•Frase.io and SurferSEO : Analyze keywords and SEO trends.

 Tip : Use ChatGPT to generate a list of topics based on your niche .

Plan An Editorial Calendar With Ai

An editorial calendar allows you to organize your publications and maintain regularity, which is essential for customer loyalty.

How can AI help?

✓ Generate content ideas over several weeks .

✓ Schedule posts in advance with WordPress or Notion.

✓ Automate social media outreach with Buffer or Hootsuite .

Example : A writer can use ChatGPT to plan a month's worth of content in a single session and optimize their strategy.

Use Templates To Write Faster

Rather than starting from scratch each time, it is possible to use reusable templates .

AI Writing Templates :

·Catchy introduction

·SEO optimized article structure (H1, H2, H3)

·Effective call to action

Tip : Jasper AI and Writesonic offer ready-made templates for writing blog posts, newsletters, and product descriptions in minutes .

4.2. Create an identity and build audience loyalty

With the rise of AI, differentiation becomes essential . An AI writer must therefore cultivate their own style to attract and retain their audience.

Developing a unique tone despite AI

One of the risks of AI is producing generic and impersonal content .

Solutions :

✓ Inject personal anecdotes into articles.

✓ Use distinctive expressions and vocabulary .

✓ Adapt your style according to the audience (humorous, formal, casual, etc.).

Example : A finance writer can stand out by making their articles accessible with simple analogies and an engaging tone .

Interact with your audience to maximize engagement

An engaged audience is more likely to share, comment, and purchase services or products.

Engagement Strategies :

·Respond to comments and messages on social media.

•Create a newsletter with exclusive content.

•Organize surveys and Q&As to better understand your audience.

Tip : Use ChatGPT to write engaging and personalized responses .

Build A Strong Personal Brand

An AI copywriter can go further by developing a recognized personal brand .

Key steps :

✓ Have a visual identity (logo, colors, typography).

✓ Publish regularly on LinkedIn, Medium, or a personal blog .

✓ Create a unique offer (example: "SEO-optimized AI writing").

Example : A writer who shares case studies and customer testimonials on his site and LinkedIn becomes a reference in his field .

4.3. Develop and diversify your sources of income

To maximize your earnings, it is essential not to limit yourself to simply writing articles .

Moving From Copywriter To Content

Consultant

Rather than just selling articles, an AI writer can offer premium services like content strategy consulting.

 Examples of premium services :

✓ SEO audits for blogs and businesses.

✓ Training on using AI in writing.

✓ Coaching for writers and entrepreneurs.

 Example : A copywriter who is proficient in SurferSEO can offer a content optimization service to businesses.

   Use AI to develop other types of services (copywriting, storytelling)

AI isn't just for blog posts: it can be used to produce impactful copywriting and engaging stories .

 Examples of services to offer :

✓ Writing sales pages and marketing emails (Copy.ai, Jasper AI).

✓ Creation of narrative content and storytelling for brands and influencers.

✓ Generation of scenarios for YouTube videos or advertisements .

 Example : An AI copywriter who is proficient in copywriting can charge several hundred euros for an optimized sales page .

Explore New Trends In Ai Writing

The world of AI is evolving rapidly, and writers need to adapt to new trends .

Trends to watch :

✔ Voice AI and conversational assistants (Google Bard, advanced ChatGPT).

✔ Interactive and personalized content .

✔ Real-time SEO optimization with AI .

Tip : Continuous training on new AI technologies and tools allows you to anticipate market developments.

Chapter Summary

✔ Increase productivity with AI through automation and writing templates.

✔ Differentiate yourself by developing a unique identity and engaging your audience .

✔ Evolve into premium services like content consulting and AI copywriting.

✔ Stay up to date on new trends to maintain a competitive edge.

PART 3: AI COMMUNITY MANAGER

Chapter 1: Automating Publications

1.1. The importance of social media management

Why an online presence is essential for a brand

Social media has become essential for any brand, business, or entrepreneur looking to increase their visibility. Proper management of these platforms allows you to:

• Increase awareness : More than 4.5 billion people use social media.

• Create an engaged community : Engaging with your audience strengthens loyalty.

• Increase sales : A good social strategy can generate conversions.

• Analyze trends : Understand public expectations and adjust your offering.

The types of content that work on each platform

Each social network has its own specificities and effective content formats:

•Facebook : Articles, long videos, discussion groups.

•Instagram : Photos, stories, short reels and attractive

visuals.

•LinkedIn : Professional content, long articles, case studies.

•Twitter (X) : Short messages, news, detailed threads.

•TikTok : Short videos, challenges, viral trends.

•YouTube : Long videos, tutorials, documentaries.

Tip : AI can automatically adapt formats to platforms to maximize engagement.

How AI can make the community manager 's job easier

Artificial intelligence automates and optimizes several key tasks:

•Content Generation : ChatGPT or Jasper can write engaging posts.

•Image and video creation : Canva AI and DALL·E make graphic design easy.

•Scheduling and posting : Tools like Buffer and Hootsuite handle automatic posting.

•Performance analysis : AI identifies the best-performing content and suggests improvements.

Result : Less time spent on daily management and more focus on strategy!

1.2. Schedule and automate posts with AI

Using tools like Buffer, Hootsuite and Metricool

Planning your posts in advance is essential for

maintaining a consistent online presence. Here are some essential tools:

•Buffer : Automatically publishes to multiple platforms.

•Hootsuite : Powerful tool with built-in performance analytics.

•Metricool : Allows you to track engagement and optimize your strategies.

Tip : These tools can be connected to ChatGPT to generate posts automatically.

Automatic generation of relevant captions and hashtags

AI helps write engaging descriptions and choose the best hashtags:

•ChatGPT : Generates optimized and attractive captions.

•Hashtagify : Find trending hashtags to reach more people.

•RiteTag : Analyzes the relevance of hashtags on each platform in real time.

Creating engaging visuals with Canva AI and Midjourney

Visuals are crucial for capturing attention. Fortunately, AI makes it possible to create images without design skills :

•Canva AI : Create professional posts in just a few clicks.

•Midjourney & DALL·E : Generate unique images from text descriptions.

Tip : Pair impactful visuals with engaging captions to maximize impact.

1.3. Maintain effortless regularity

Develop an AI editorial calendar

An editorial calendar helps organize and plan publications in advance. AI can:

•Suggest the best times to post based on audience.

•Generate content ideas based on current trends.

•Automate reminders so you never miss a post.

Schedule content in advance

Scheduling content for a month or more ensures consistent presence effortlessly.

Use a mix of AI tools (ChatGPT, Canva, Hootsuite) to automate the entire process.

Automatically adapt posts to current trends

AI algorithms analyze trends in real time to adapt content:

•Google Trends : Identifies popular topics.

•BuzzSumo : Spots viral content on the web.

•Metricool AI : Adjusts publications based on market developments.

Tip : Incorporate references to current events and trends to boost engagement.

Chapter Summary

✓ AI can automate social media management and save time.

✓ Planning and scheduling your posts ensures consistent presence effortlessly.

✓ Using AI tools like ChatGPT, Canva AI, and Buffer helps maximize the impact of your posts.

Chapter 2: Interacting With Subscribers Using Ai

2.1. Reply to messages and comments with AI

Use of chatbots (ManyChat , Chatfuel)

Quick interaction with subscribers is essential to maintain a good relationship with your audience. AI chatbots allow you to respond to messages automatically and efficiently .

Popular tools :

•ManyChat : Ideal for Facebook Messenger, Instagram, and WhatsApp . Allows you to automate responses to frequently asked questions.

•Chatfuel : A leader in creating bots without coding, perfect for interacting with subscribers 24/7.

•Drift & MobileMonkey : Specializing in customer interactions and lead generation.

Example : A chatbot can immediately answer

common product questions, share links, or direct the user to human customer service if needed.

Generating personalized automatic responses

Subscribers prefer natural interactions over robotic responses. AI allows you to:

✓ Analyze the message and offer a contextual response .

✓ Adapt the tone according to the situation (professional or friendly response).

✓ Automate welcome or thank you messages after an interaction.

Recommended tools :

·ChatGPT + API : Allows you to train a bot to respond in a personalized way.

·Zendesk AI & Crisp Chat : Professional tools for managing customer interactions.

Filter and prioritize important messages

When receiving hundreds of messages and comments , AI can help:

·Detect urgent messages (e.g. customer complaint, request for collaboration).

·Highlight high-engagement comments for better visibility.

·Filter spam or toxic messages automatically.

Useful AI tools :

·Meta Business Suite (Facebook & Instagram):

Automatically prioritizes messages.

•Sprinklr & Sprout Social : Advanced analytics to filter and respond to important messages.

2.2. Analyze engagement and adapt your strategy

Tracking post performance with AI (Meta Business Suite, Sprout Social)

Why is this important?

Engagement analysis helps you understand which types of content work best and optimize your strategy.

Recommended tools :

•Meta Business Suite : Provides detailed insights on Facebook & Instagram.

•Sprout Social : Analyzes interactions across multiple platforms and offers AI recommendations.

•Hootsuite Analytics : Generates automatic reports on engagement trends.

Example : AI can suggest adjusting the frequency of publication or prioritizing a specific type of content (video, carousel, stories).

Identifying the best posting times

AI analyzes follower engagement history and behaviors to recommend the best posting times .

Effective tools :

•Later & Metricool : Suggest optimal times to post on Instagram and TikTok.

•CoSchedule : Analyzes interactions and adjusts posting times accordingly.

 Tip : Posting at the right time can increase reach by 50% to 100% on some networks.

Adjusting tone and style based on audience feedback

AI analyzes comments and interactions to understand how audiences perceive posts.

✔ If followers respond better to humorous posts , AI can suggest adopting a lighter tone.

✔ If topics generate negative reactions , it can suggest avoiding certain themes.

✔ AI helps test different approaches and adjust content based on feedback .

 AI tools to analyze tone :

•MonkeyLearn : Analyzes the sentiments of comments and posts.

•Talkwalker : Monitors brand reputation by analyzing audience reactions.

2.3. Managing a community without spending too much time on it

Automatic comment moderation (ChatGPT, Facebook AI)

Moderation is essential to maintaining a healthy space on your networks. AI can:

✓ Delete inappropriate or aggressive comments . ✓ Filter hateful or spam messages .

✓ Automatically respond to recurring questions.

Recommended tools :

•Facebook & Instagram AI : Automatically detects and hides offensive comments.

•Jasper AI : Generates polite responses to sensitive comments.

•ChatGPT + Zapier : Can automate custom moderations.

Tip : Set blocked keywords to avoid harmful content under your posts.

Identify and delete spam or inappropriate messages

AI can automatically spot and remove :

•Messages containing fraudulent links .

•Repetitive comments or advertising bots .

•Personal attacks and hate speech.

AI Anti-Spam Tools :

•Nightbot & Automod (Twitch , YouTube) : Blocks spam and live trolls.

•Hive Moderation : Advanced AI for detecting inappropriate content.

Create a close relationship with your audience using AI

AI helps personalize the subscriber experience by:

✓ Sending them automated messages after an interaction.

✓ Creating tailored responses based on each individual's preferences.

✓ Segmenting the audience to deliver content tailored to each group.

Example of AI tools to improve audience engagement :

•HubSpot & ActiveCampaign : Create personalized message sequences.

•Tidio Chatbot : Answers questions and directs visitors to suitable offers.

Tip : Use AI- collected data to understand your community's expectations and deliver more engaging content .

Chapter Summary

✓ Automate responses and comments with AI chatbots to save time.

✓ Analyze engagement with AI to optimize your content strategy.

✓ Using AI to moderate and secure your online space.

✓ Personalize interactions to strengthen the relationship with subscribers.

Chapter 3: Ai Tools To Maximize Engagement

3.1. Generate engaging content with AI

Creation of infographics and short videos with AI

Visual content attracts more attention and generates more engagement than simple text. AI facilitates the rapid and efficient creation of visuals and videos:

Recommended tools :

•Canva AI : Generates impactful infographics and visuals in just a few clicks.

•Pictory & InVideo AI : Create short videos from texts or articles.

•Lumen5 : Transforms articles into engaging videos.

Tip : Add automatic captions with Descript to maximize video engagement.

Generating ideas for viral posts

AI can suggest content ideas tailored to your audience by analyzing current trends.

Useful AI tools :

•ChatGPT & Jasper AI : Generate engaging post concepts.

•BuzzSumo : Identifies the most shared trends and topics on social networks.

•AnswerThePublic : Detects questions that Internet users ask.

Example : A brand can use AI to find current trends on

TikTok and tailor its content accordingly.

Storytelling and copywriting optimized with AI

Good storytelling boosts engagement and builds subscriber loyalty. AI helps:

✔ Write engaging captions with Copy.ai & Writesonic .

✔ Create impactful video scripts in seconds.

✔ Optimize descriptions for trending keywords .

Recommended Tools :

•ChatGPT & Jasper : Ideal for impactful copywriting.

•Headlime : Generates catchy headlines optimized for engagement.

•Persado AI : Optimizes marketing campaigns with storytelling based on consumer psychology.

 Tip : Test different versions of a post to see which one performs best in engagement (A/B testing).

3.2. Advertising and smart targeting with AI

Using AI to optimize advertising campaigns (Facebook Ads, Google Ads)

AI improves campaign performance by automating optimization and offering real-time adjustments.

AI Advertising Tools :

•Adzooma & Revealbot : Automatically optimize Google Ads and Facebook Ads campaigns.

•Phrasee AI : Generates high-performing ad copy based on best practice analysis.

•Albert AI : Complete automation of advertising campaigns.

 Example : An e-commerce company can use Adzooma to increase its conversion rate by adjusting bids and targeting in real time.

Automatic audience segmentation and targeting

AI analyzes user behaviors and preferences to better target ads.

AI tools for targeting :

•Facebook Lookalike Audiences : Finds audiences similar to existing customers.

•Google Smart Bidding : Automatically adjusts bids to maximize return on investment.

•   Customer AI (Salesforce) : Predictions based on customer behavior.

 Tip : Use lookalike audiences to reach prospects with the same interests as your current customers .

Real-time performance analysis and optimization

AI allows advertising campaigns to be automatically adjusted based on real-time performance.

AI analysis tools :

•Hootsuite Ads : Optimizes campaigns and offers real-time recommendations.

•Optmyzr : Analyzes Google Ads performance and adjusts bidding strategies.

•Google Analytics 4 : Built-in AI to detect trends and adjust ad targeting.

Tip : Set up AI alerts to automatically adjust ads if performance drops.

3.3. Developing a strong brand through AI

Create a coherent and impactful visual identity

AI can help you create a unique brand identity so your brand is instantly recognizable.

AI tools for visual identity :

•Looka & Brandmark : Generate logos and color palettes tailored to your brand.

•Khroma AI : Suggests color combinations based on visual psychology.

•RunwayML & Deep Dream Generator : Create unique and artistic visuals for a strong identity.

Tip : Make sure all your posts follow the same aesthetic for better brand consistency.

Automate competitive analysis and learn from trends

AI helps analyze competitors and identify trends to follow.

AI tools for competitive analysis :

•Crimson Hexagon & Brandwatch : Monitor

competitor strategies in real-time.

•Google Trends & Exploding Topics : Identify emerging trends before they go viral.

•Sprout Social : Compare competitor engagement and performance.

Example : A startup can use Google Trends to anticipate trending topics and publish content before the competition.

Personalize content to retain subscribers

AI makes it possible to offer ultra-personalized experiences to subscribers to build loyalty.

AI tools for personalization :

•Dynamic Yield : Recommends content tailored to user preferences.

•Persado AI : Personalizes marketing messages based on the target audience's emotions.

•Adobe Sensei : Optimizes user experience with AI recommendations.

Example : A blog can use Dynamic Yield to show different articles based on each visitor's interests .

Chapter Summary

✓ Generate engaging content with AI graphics and video creation tools.

✓ Optimize ad campaigns with automated targeting and tracking.

✓ Develop a strong brand by automating competitive analysis and content personalization.

Chapter 4: Becoming A Profitable Ai Community Manager

4.1. Finding clients and setting prices

Freelance: where to offer your services?

Becoming a community manager specializing in AI is a growing market . Here are the platforms where you can offer your freelance services:

General platforms :

•Upwork & Fiverr : Ideal for finding one-off assignments.

•Malt : Preferred European platform for professionals.

•PeoplePerHour : Focused on digital services.

Specialized platforms :

•Toptal : For digital strategy experts.

•Kolabtree : For AI and advanced marketing consultants.

•Freelancer.com : Wide range of digital opportunities.

Tip : Create an attractive profile with case studies and examples of results achieved using AI.

Strategies to stand out and demonstrate your AI expertise

✓ Highlight your AI tools : Mention your skills with ChatGPT, Jasper, ManyChat , Canva AI, Hootsuite , Adzooma , etc.

✓ Publish educational content : Write LinkedIn or Medium articles about using AI in social media management.

✓ Offer a free audit : Offer AI analysis of social networks to convince your first customers.

✓ Create an AI Portfolio : Show concrete examples of publications created with AI and their results.

Determine your prices based on the services offered

Here is a basis for structuring your rates:

Basic services :

•AI social media management (3-4 posts/week) → €300-500/month

•AI moderation (via chatbots and automations) → €200-400/month

•Creation of AI-optimized content (posts, infographics, videos) → €100/post

Advanced services :

•AI digital strategy + automated advertising → €800-1500/month

•Creation and management of an AI chatbot for engagement → €500-1200

•Audit and optimization of an AI digital presence → €400-1000

Tip : Charge in bundles to increase your perceived value. Example:

AI management pack + moderation + targeted advertising = €1,500/month instead of €2,000 à la carte.

4.2. Create and sell automated offers

Offer AI-assisted social media management packages

You can offer packaged offers where everything is automated thanks to AI :

✓ "Starter" Pack → Automated creation and publication (€500/month)

✓ "Growth" Pack → Addition of AI moderation and advertising management (€1000/month)

✓ "Expert" Pack → Complete strategy with advanced AI reporting (€2,000/month)

Recommended automation tools :

•Zapier : Automates publishing across multiple platforms.

•Hootsuite & Buffer : AI Scheduling and Analysis.

•Adzooma : Automatic ad optimization.

Tip : Offer a one- month trial at a discounted price to attract your first customers.

Sell AI templates and strategies for businesses and influencers

AI allows you to create profitable digital products :

Ideas for saleable products :

•AI-powered Instagram post templates (30 templates → €50)

•AI Chatbot User Guide for Business (PDF 30 pages → €100)

•Boost AI Engagement" strategy (Detailed action plan → €200-500)

Where to sell these products?

•On Gumroad , Etsy , Podia or your own site.

•On Kajabi if you want to add additional training.

Example : An AI CM can sell a pack of 50 Instagram post templates with AI for €100 to 200 clients , generating €20,000 without additional work .

Automate reports and analyses to build customer loyalty

AI can generate ultra-detailed reports effortlessly.

Recommended tools :

•Google Data Studio : Create automatic visual reports.

•Sprout Social & Hootsuite Analytics : Performance analysis and AI suggestions.

•Metricool : AI reporting for social media and advertising.

Tip : Charge extra for sending custom AI reports each month (+100 to 500€/month).

4.3. Evolve and diversify its services

Moving from community management to digital AI strategy

Companies are looking for experts who can integrate AI into their overall marketing strategy . You can progress to:

✓ AI Consultant in Digital Strategy (Billing: €2,000-5,000/project)

✓ AI Advertising Specialist (Facebook Ads, Google Ads automated)

✓ AI SEO Expert (AI Optimization and Content for Google)

Tip : Offer internal training to companies to monetize your knowledge.

Offer AI training for businesses

Businesses want to learn how to use AI to optimize their communication . You can sell:

✓ Online training (Udemy, Teachable , Kajabi)

✓ Corporate workshops on AI applied to marketing

✓ 1:1 Coaching on AI-assisted digital management

Recommended rates :

•Online training "AI & Community Management" → €99-499

•AI coaching (3 sessions x 1 hour) → €500-1000

•AI business workshop (1 day) → €1,500-5,000

Example : Selling 100 places at €299 on an AI training course = €29,900 in turnover ⬜.

Anticipating developments in digital marketing with AI

AI is evolving fast, and staying up-to-date is a major asset . To differentiate yourself:

✓ Monitor AI trends through sites like AI Business & Future Tools .

✓ Test new AI solutions as soon as they are released (Ex: Google Gemini, OpenAI Updates).

✓ Join AI growth hacking communities (Reddit, Discord, Slack).

Tip : Develop your personal brand by posting regular insights on LinkedIn or YouTube.

Chapter Summary

✓ Find freelance clients and set your prices according to your AI services.

✓ Create automated offers and sell profitable digital products .

✓ Move towards consulting, training and AI digital strategy .

PART 4: AI VIDEO MAKER (NO EDITING)

Chapter 1: Creating Videos Without Technical Skills

1.1. Why is video the dominant format on the Internet?

The rise of video content on YouTube, TikTok, Instagram and Facebook

Video content has exploded in recent years:

✓ YouTube : Over 500 hours of videos uploaded every minute.

✓ TikTok : Ultra-powerful algorithm favoring short and viral videos.

✓ Instagram & Facebook : Strong emphasis on Reels and Stories .

Why this success?

•Ease of consumption : A video captures attention faster than text.

•Better engagement : A user retains 95% of a video message compared to 10% when reading a text.

•Format favored by algorithms : Platforms boost the visibility of videos compared to images and text.

The impact of videos on engagement and monetization

More views = More interactions = More money!

Creators use video to:

✓ Boost engagement (likes, shares, comments)

✓ Monetize via YouTube Ads, TikTok Creator Fund or Instagram Reels Play

✓ Sell digital products (training courses, ebooks, subscriptions)

✓ Attracting sponsors and partnerships

Concrete examples :

·A YouTuber with 100,000 views/month can earn between €500 and €2,000 in advertising.

·A TikToker with 1M views/month can generate between €200 and €1000 via the Creator Fund .

·An Instagram influencer can charge €1,000 to €5,000 per sponsored collaboration .

How AI is making video creation accessible to everyone

With AI, no more editing skills needed!

·Automatic generation : Tools like Synthesia or Pictory create videos from text.

·Simplified editing : AI can add subtitles, transitions and effects with one click.

·Realistic AI Voiceovers : No need to record your own voice.

Conclusion : Today, anyone can create video content and profit from it, even if they are not an editor or videographer.

1.2. AI tools to create videos easily

Synthesia: Create videos with animated AI avatars

Synthesia.io allows you to:

✓ Transform text into video with a realistic talking avatar . ✓ Generate an AI voiceover in more than 120 languages .

✓ Create professional videos without a camera or microphone .

Ideal for :

•Make explanatory or tutorial videos .

•Present products and services in a professional manner.

•Automate the creation of marketing videos .

☐ InVideo and Pictory : Automatically transform text into video

InVideo.io and Pictory.ai offer:

✓ Ready-to-use templates (corporate , storytelling, social media).

✓ Convert texts to videos in just a few clicks .

✓ Automatic addition of AI voice, subtitles and animations .

Ideal for :

•Turn blog posts into YouTube videos .

•Create content for TikTok, Instagram or Facebook quickly .

•Generate videos without complex editing .

 Runway ML and HeyGen : Video generation and editing made easy

 Runway ML :

✓ Automatic background removal without green screen.

✓ AI special effects to give a professional look.

✓ Video animation and enhancement with AI .

 HeyGen :

✓ Create a talking AI avatar by customizing its appearance and voice .

✓ Automatic translation of videos into multiple languages .

✓ Ideal for multilingual content on social media .

 Example of use :

An entrepreneur can use HeyGen to make promotional videos in English and French without recording multiple times .

1.3. Produce a video in minutes with AI

 Choose a topic and structure its content

Before creating a video, you need a clear and engaging topic :

✔ Set a goal (educate, entertain, sell).

✔ Choose a format (short TikTok video, YouTube tutorial, professional presentation).

✔ Structure your script :

·Impactful introduction

·Development with key points

·Final call to action (CTA)

Example AI script for a YouTube video :

"Did you know you can create a video without technical skills? Today I'm going to show you how to generate professional videos with AI in less than 5 minutes!"

Generate a video in a few clicks with an AI tool

1 Write a text or import an article .

2 Choose an AI video template (Synthesia, InVideo , Pictory).

3 Add an AI voice or animated avatar .

4 Customize the visual elements (colors, font, music) .

5 Let AI generate the video in seconds!

Example :

A business coach can convert a blog post into a YouTube video using Pictory , then publish it automatically.

Customize elements for a professional look

Elements to customize :

✓ Eye-catching title in large format.

✓ Dynamic subtitles to improve readability.

✓ Smooth animations and transitions to capture attention.

✓ Royalty-free background music to liven up the video.

Examples of tools to improve rendering :

•Canva Pro : Adding Graphic Elements.

•CapCut AI : Simplified editing with trendy effects.

•Description : AI-powered audio and video editing.

Bonus : Add smart CTAs (subscribe, link in bio, interactive comment).

Chapter Summary

✓ Video is the dominant format , favored by platforms and the algorithm.

✓ AI makes video creation accessible to everyone , without the need for technical skills.

✓ Tools like Synthesia, Pictory or InVideo allow you to create videos in just a few clicks .

✓ Good structuring and customization allow for a professional result in minimal time.

Chapter 2: Script Generation And Voiceover With Ai

2.1. Write an impactful script with ChatGPT

Find viral content ideas

The most popular videos follow proven trends and formats :

✓ Current Trends : Analysis of popular topics via Google Trends, TikTok Discover, and YouTube Trends.

✓ Engaging formats : Lists, challenges, comparisons, storytelling, analyses.

✓ Using AI : Ask ChatGPT:

•"Give me 5 ideas for viral YouTube videos about artificial intelligence."

•"What are the trending topics on TikTok right now?"

Example of ideas generated by AI :

•"How can AI replace your job in 2025?"

•"Top 5 Free AI Apps to Try Now"

•"The AI wrote this script… and here is the result!"

Generate a structured and engaging script

A good script follows a simple structure:

1 Hook (5 seconds max) : Ask an intriguing question or make a shocking statement.

2 Development : Breaks down the subject into clear and rhythmic points.

3 Call-to-action (CTA) : Asks to like , comment, subscribe, click on a link.

Example prompt for ChatGPT :

"Write a compelling YouTube script on 'The 3 Best AI Tools for Editing Videos Fast'. Use a dynamic and approachable tone."

Example of script generated by ChatGPT :

"Did you know you can create a professional video in 5 minutes... without any technical skills? Today, I'm showing you the 3 best AI tools to revolutionize your video creation!"

Adapt the style according to the platform

Each platform has its own rules:

YouTube : Long videos (8-15 min), storytelling, impactful thumbnails.

TikTok / Instagram Reels : Ultra-short videos (15-60 sec), dynamism, on-screen text.

LinkedIn / Facebook : Educational content, more traditional format, professional tone.

Example of adaptation of the same script :

YouTube : "We're going to take a look at the best AI tools for creating viral content in 2024. Stay tuned until the end, I have a bonus for you!"

TikTok : " ⬜ Want to save time on your edits? Here are 3 AI tools to try NOW! ⬜ "

2.2. Create a professional voiceover with AI

Using tools like ElevenLabs, Murf AI and PlayHT

ElevenLabs : Ultra-realistic AI voices, ability to clone a voice.

Murf AI : Ideal for natural and expressive voiceovers.

PlayHT : Voiceover generation in several languages with customizable intonations.

Example workflow with Murf AI :

1 Copy and paste your script.

2 Choose a voice from several styles (male, female, dynamic, serious).

3 Adjust the pitch, speed, and intonation.

4 Download the audio and embed it into the video.

✔ Customize tone and vocal style

AI allows you to adapt your voice to the context:

✔ Dynamic and engaging voice for TikTok.

✔ Calm and professional voice for online training.

✔ Emotive and immersive voice for storytelling.

✔ Example prompt for ElevenLabs :

"Generate a French voiceover for an AI tutorial with an enthusiastic and accessible tone."

✔ Automatic integration of voiceover into the video

✔ Recommended software :

✔ InVideo : Automatically combines script, AI voice, and visuals.

✔ Description : Allows you to edit audio and synchronize voice with video.

✓ Adobe Premiere Pro AI : Generates automatic subtitles and adjusts voiceover.

✓ Save time : Some tools directly synchronize the voiceover with the animations.

2.3. Add automatic subtitles and effects

✓ Automatic subtitling with Kapwing and Descript

✓ Kapwing : Automatically add stylish captions for TikTok/YouTube Shorts.

✓ Description : Edit text and audio at the same time (corrects speech errors).

Why add subtitles?

•85% of videos are watched without sound on social media.

•Improves SEO and understanding.

Example of use with Kapwing :

1 Import your video.

2 Activate automatic transcription.

3 Modify the subtitles to make them more readable.

4 Export with a striking design.

Automatic generation of transitions and animations

AI tools to boost your videos :

✓ Runway ML : Generates AI visual effects and animations.

✔ Veed.io : Creates text animations and automatic transitions.

✔ CapCut AI : Applies trendy filters and effects with one click.

Example workflow with Veed.io :

1 Download the raw video.

2 Enable the "AI Animations" option.

3 Customize transitions and effects.

4 Export in high quality for TikTok or YouTube Shorts.

Format optimization for mobile and desktop

Adapt your video to the right format depending on the platform :

✔ TikTok, Instagram Reels, YouTube Shorts : Vertical format (9:16) .

✔ YouTube, Facebook, LinkedIn : Horizontal format (16:9) .

AI tools to automatically adapt the format :

✔ Kapwing Auto Resize : Converts horizontal video to vertical.

✔ InShot : Adds margins and crops automatically.

Best practices :

•Place the text at the top or center to avoid it being hidden by the interface.

·Add dynamic captioning and emojis to maximize impact .

Chapter Summary

✓ A good script is the foundation of a successful video : ChatGPT helps structure and optimize viral content.

✓ AI voiceovers (ElevenLabs, Murf AI, PlayHT) make the process faster and more professional.

✓ Tools like Kapwing and Descript make it easy to automatically add subtitles and effects.

✓ Optimizing your videos for each platform ensures better engagement.

Chapter 3: Monetizing Your Videos (Youtube, Social Networks, Etc.)

3.1. Making Money with YouTube and AI

Monetization through the YouTube Partner Program

YouTube allows you to generate revenue through its YouTube Partner Program (YPP) . To be eligible:

✓ 1,000 subscribers minimum.

✓ 4,000 hours of viewing (or 10M views on Shorts in 90 days).

✓ Comply with YouTube's monetization rules.

YouTube Revenue Sources :

•Advertisements (AdSense): CPM varying between $1 and $20 depending on the niche.

•Super Cats & Stickers (during live shows).

•Paid Subscriptions : Exclusive content for members.

•YouTube Shopping : Selling products through YouTube.

•Affiliation and partnerships : Income via tracked links .

Optimization to earn more :

•High CPM Niche : Finance, Tech, AI, Online Training.

•Long videos (+8 min) : Allows you to insert more ads.

•Eye-catching thumbnails and titles to maximize click-through rate.

Using AI to create consistent, optimized content

AI makes it easier to produce monetizable videos quickly and efficiently .

 Automated workflow with AI :

1 Script generation → ChatGPT (ideas, structures, CTAs).

2 AI Voiceover → ElevenLabs, Murf AI (natural voices).

3 Assisted editing → Descript, Runway ML, InVideo .

4 AI Thumbnails → Canva, Midjourney, DALL-E (automatic thumbnail creation).

5 SEO optimized → TubeBuddy , VidIQ (keywords,

tags, descriptions).

YouTube Automation Example :

•Use Pictory AI to turn an article into a YouTube video.

•Generate a voiceover and add AI visuals in 10 minutes .

•Schedule and publish 10 videos per week at an optimized cadence.

 Tips to increase retention rate and subscribers

The secret to boosting your audience and maximizing your earnings:

  Maximum Retention = YouTube boosts videos watched to completion.

✔ Powerful hook from the first 5 seconds.

✔ Dynamic chaptering to keep attention.

✔ Fast editing (frequent cuts , effects, zooms).

✔ Natural calls to action (ask the audience a question).

✔ Incentive to subscribe via an exclusive bonus (PDF, training, etc.).

 Example of an optimized YouTube script :

"Do you want to make money with AI? Today, I'm going to show you how to automate your videos and generate passive income on YouTube... stay tuned until the end, I have a surprise for you!"

3.2. Monetize your content on TikTok,

Instagram and Facebook

How platform compensation programs work

TikTok Creator Fund (from 10K subscribers and 100K views/month).

Instagram Reels Bonus (by invitation, based on engagement).

Facebook Reels Play (pay per views and interactions).

Other sources of income :

•Sponsoring (partnerships with brands).

•Affiliation (links tracked on bio and stories).

•Digital products (training, ebooks, templates).

Creation of videos adapted to each social network

TikTok & Instagram Reels : Short videos (15-60 sec), 9:16 vertical format, fast pace.

Facebook Reels : More storytelling content, captions, engagement in comments.

AI tools to create engaging content :

•CapCut AI : Fast editing and dynamic effects.

•Synthesia AI : Creating AI avatars for educational videos.

•Reels AI Tools : Automatic generation of trending hashtags and music.

Example of a video optimized for TikTok :

" This AI turns your voice into that of a famous

actor... Here's how to use it!"

Strategies to maximize engagement and virality

✓ 3-second

hard-hitting hook . ✓ Viral trends and sounds (TikTok, Instagram Trends).

✓ Interactive content (surveys, challenges, questions).

✓ Regular publication (3-5 videos/week).

Tip: Recycle the contents

•Turn a YouTube video into multiple TikToks /Reels.

•Use AI to edit text and editing styles.

3.3. *Selling AI videos and services as a freelancer*

Offer automated videos for businesses and influencers

✓ Creation of explainer videos (SaaS, startups).

✓ Content generation for YouTube/TikTok influencers.

✓ Automated editing for social networks.

Recommended tools :

•Runway ML → AI Effects and Animations.

•Synthesia AI → Explanatory videos with AI avatars.

•Pictory AI → Transforming articles into videos.

Offer AI video packages on Fiverr and Upwork

Examples of services for sale :

✓ Turnkey TikTok/Reels video creation (with AI voice and editing).

✓ Automated YouTube content generation .

✓ AI ad editing for e-commerce.

Fiverr ad example :

"I create YouTube and TikTok videos with AI, optimized for virality!"

Price of services :

·Pack of 10 TikTok AI videos : €100-300.

·AI explanatory video: €50-150 .

·Full AI YouTube video: €200-500 .

Create an AI-assisted video production agency

Scalable business model :

✓ Automation with AI → Cost reduction.

✓ Creation of video packages for businesses.

✓ Subscription offers for regular content.

Example of an AI agency offer :

·Social Media Pack : 30 short videos/month = €1,500 .

·Automated YouTube : 4 long videos / month = €2,500 .

Growth Strategy :

✓ Prospect on LinkedIn and Instagram.

✓ Publish case studies and testimonials.

✓ Automate production with AI tools.

Chapter Summary

✓ YouTube, TikTok, Instagram, and Facebook offer several ways to monetize your content with AI.

✓ AI enables video production at scale and automates the process.

✓ Freelancing and AI video agencies are lucrative opportunities.

Chapter 4: Optimizing Your Ai Video Creator Business

4.1. Increasing productivity with AI

Schedule and automate video creation

AI helps automate and speed up video production, reducing the time needed for each creation.

Effective production strategy :

1 Creating an editorial calendar → Using Notion or Trello.

2 Automation of repetitive tasks → AI for scripting, voice, editing.

3 Video Scheduling → Schedule posts with Metricool or Hootsuite .

Useful tools :

•ChatGPT → Generate ideas and scripts.

•Synthesia / ElevenLabs → Automated voiceover.

•Pictory AI → Transform text into video.

•CapCut / Descript → Quick editing and automatic subtitles.

Recycle written content into videos with AI

Instead of creating content from scratch , AI can automatically transform articles, tweets or newsletters into videos .

Example workflow :

✔ Transform a blog post into a video script with ChatGPT.

✔ Generate an animated video with Pictory AI .

✔ Post a clip on TikTok/Reels to maximize visibility.

Tip: Convert a podcast or interview into multiple short videos for Instagram and TikTok.

Generate multiple videos in a single working session

Batch Recording + AI = Maximum Time Saving

Instead of creating 1 video per day , produce 10 videos in a single session .

Effective method :

1 Quickly write multiple scripts with ChatGPT .

2 Batch AI voiceover recording with ElevenLabs .

3 Editing and automatic generation with Pictory AI or Runway ML .

4 Scheduling posts with Buffer or Hootsuite .

Result : 1 day of work = 1 month of programmed content .

4.2. Building a brand and building audience loyalty

Create a unique style despite AI

AI makes production easier, but the human touch makes the difference .

How to personalize your content?

✓ Choose a specific niche (finance, tech, motivation, business).

✓ Create a unique visual identity (thumbnails , colors, typography).

✓ Develop a distinctive voice or tone (even with an AI voice).

✓ Add personal elements (anecdotes, storytelling).

Tip : Mix human voice + AI for a strong identity.

Engage your audience with interactive formats

Strategies to increase engagement :

✓ Ask questions in videos.

✓ Conduct polls and Q&As on YouTube and Instagram.

✓ Create episodic series (e.g., "The Secrets of Millionaire Entrepreneurs").

✓ Respond to comments with short videos .

AI Engagement Example : Generate a personalized video summary for each popular comment.

Use data analysis to improve your content

Analysis tools to use :

✓ YouTube Analytics → See click-through rates, watch time.

✓ VidIQ / TubeBuddy → Optimize SEO and keywords.

✓ TikTok / Instagram Insights → Analyze best posting times.

AI Strategy :

·Use ChatGPT to analyze trends and adjust content accordingly.

·Test different video formats and see which ones perform best.

4.3. Exploring new opportunities in AI video

Start an automated YouTube channel (cash cow)

The YouTube Cash Cow Model: Create 100% automated channels , without appearing on screen.

Steps to an automated AI YouTube channel :

1 Choose a profitable niche (finance, motivation, tech, cryptos).

2 Generate scripts with ChatGPT .

3 Create an AI voiceover with ElevenLabs .

4 Edit video with Pictory AI or InVideo .

5 Publish and optimize with VidIQ and TubeBuddy .

Profitability : A monetized channel can generate €2,000-10,000/month passively.

Experimenting with augmented reality and generative AI

The future of videos is AI and augmented reality .

Opportunities to test :

✓ Use Runway ML to create advanced visual effects .

✓ Test AI avatar generation with Synthesia .

✓ Experiment with interactive AR videos for Instagram/TikTok.

Trend 2025: Immersive and hyper-personalized videos with AI.

Anticipating the evolution of artificial intelligence in video

What the future holds :

✓ YouTube and TikTok will further promote AI videos .

✓ Generative AI will enable ultra-realistic videos in 1 click .

✓ New platforms and tools will emerge (eg: Meta AI Video).

 Winning strategy : Be a pioneer and adopt new AI trends before everyone else .

Chapter Summary

✓ Optimize your productivity with AI to produce more content quickly.

✓ Stand out by bringing a unique and human touch.

✓ Analyze your performance and adjust your strategy.

✓ Explore new opportunities like YouTube Cash Cow and augmented reality.

Chapter 1: Creating Logos And Visuals With Ai

1.1 Why is graphic design essential?

The Importance of Visuals for Brands and Businesses

In a world where consumer attention is increasingly in demand, impactful design is essential to capture interest and strengthen a brand's visual identity. Whether for a business, an entrepreneur, or a content creator, good design:

✔ Reinforces a brand's credibility and professionalism

✔ Improves recognition and memorability among audiences

✔ Boosts engagement on social media and marketing materials

The most requested types of creations

Artificial intelligence now makes it possible to quickly produce high-quality visuals. Here are the most popular types of creations:

Logos : Visual identity of a company or project

Banners : For websites, blogs and social media pages

Social media posts : Instagram, Facebook, TikTok, LinkedIn, etc. posts.

Posters and flyers : Communication materials for events or promotions

Business cards and professional documents

How is AI revolutionizing graphic design?

Artificial intelligence has transformed the graphic design process by making design:

Accessible : No design skills are required to create professional visuals

Fast : Automatic generation of logos, illustrations and banners in minutes

Customizable : Ability to adjust colors, fonts, and styles with AI suggestions

1.2 Generate a professional logo with AI

The best AI tools to create a logo in just a few clicks

There are several platforms that allow you to generate quality logos in just a few minutes:

Looka (looka.com) – Professional logo creation with artificial intelligence

Brandmark (brandmark.io) – Automatic generation with choice of styles and icons

AI Logo (logoai.com) – Advanced customization and adaptation to the graphic charter

Steps to Create a Logo with AI

1 Select an AI tool – For example, Looka or Logo AI

2 Enter the name of the company or project

3 Choose a style (modern, minimalist, classic, etc.)

4 Customize colors, fonts and icons

5 Download the logo in high resolution

Tip : For a truly unique logo, combine AI creation with a little manual tweaking via Canva or Photoshop.

1.3 Creation of visuals for social networks and marketing

Using AI to automatically generate images and illustrations

AI makes it possible to create ultra-realistic or stylized images without graphic design skills. Here are some powerful tools:

Canva AI – Automatic generation of ready-to-use designs

Midjourney – Creation of artistic illustrations and images

Runway ML – Retouching and improving visuals via AI

Optimize your visuals for each platform

Each social network has its own image formats. Here are the ideal dimensions:

• Instagram Post : 1080 x 1080 px

Instagram Story / Reels : 1080 x 1920 px

Facebook Cover : 820 x 312 px

LinkedIn Post : 1200 x 627 px

Automate multi-format creation : Tools like Canva AI allow you to automatically adapt a creation to multiple formats.

·Adapting a design for different media

·can generate variations suitable for various media (posters, business cards, flyers). Example:

✓ Create an Instagram post with Canva AI

✓ Automatically generate a version for an Instagram story

✓ Adapt the visual for a printable flyer

·Conclusion: AI, a powerful asset for graphic design

·Thanks to artificial intelligence, graphic design is more accessible than ever. Whether you're an entrepreneur, freelancer, or content creator, you can now generate impactful designs in minutes.

· Logos and visuals are essential for a brand

AI tools help create professional content quickly

Adapting your creations to multiple media maximizes their impact

Chapter 2: Using Tools Like Midjourney And Canva Ai

Artificial intelligence has revolutionized graphic design by making creation faster, more intuitive, and more accessible to everyone. Whether you're an entrepreneur, graphic designer, or content creator, these tools will allow you to generate professional visuals in just a few clicks.

2.1. Midjourney: Creating artistic images with AI

How Midjourney works and image generation by prompt

Midjourney is a generative AI that creates artistic illustrations and images from simple text descriptions called prompts . Accessible via Discord , it works by entering a text description of the desired image.

How to use Midjourney?

1 Join the Midjourney Discord server and subscribe to a paid plan

2 Type the command /imagine followed by a detailed description

3 Let the AI generate multiple versions of the image

4 Select, enhance, or enlarge the final image

Optimized prompts to achieve professional visuals

A well-formulated prompt improves the quality and relevance of the generated images.

Example of an effective prompt:

Basic : "A lion in the jungle"

Optimized : "A majestic golden lion in a lush jungle, cinematic lighting, ultra detailed, realistic style – ar 16:9 –v 5"

Tips for powerful prompts :

Precision : Add details (style, colors, mood, perspective)

Formatting : Specify an aspect ratio (eg: – ar 16:9 for widescreen)

AI Version : Add –v 5 for latest Midjourney update

Examples of applications

is ideal for creating:

✓ Unique advertising posters and banners

✓ Artistic illustrations for books and blogs

✓ Graphic concepts for brands and products

2.2. Canva AI: Graphic design made easy

Pre-designed templates and design automation

Canva AI is a turnkey solution for creating visuals in minutes. It offers:

Thousands of templates for posters, social posts, presentations

Built-in AI that automatically adjusts colors, fonts, and alignments

An intuitive editor to customize each element

Use Canva AI in 3 easy steps :

1 Choose a template from those offered by Canva

2 Personalize with your text, images and colors

3 Export in high definition for printing or publication

Adding text, animations and AI effects

Canva offers several AI-powered features :

Dynamic text effects (shadow, outline, animation)

Automatic background removal

AI image generation directly in the interface

Ideal for :

✓ Instagram, Facebook and LinkedIn posts

✓ Presentations and professional documents

✓ Stories and animated videos

Instant collaboration and edits for clients

Canva makes teamwork easier thanks to:

Online file sharing with real-time comments

Quick editing without complex software

Multi-format export (PNG, PDF, MP4, etc.)

2.3. Other AI tools for graphics

Adobe Firefly: AI image generation and editing

Adobe Firefly lets you generate and edit images using AI in Photoshop and Illustrator.

Key Features :

✓ Image generation from text

✓ Element replacement and smart fill

✓ Seamless integration with Adobe Suite

Runway ML: AI video and animation creation

Runway ML is a platform specialized in AI video editing and generation .

Recommended use for :

✓ AI animations and special effects

✓ Background replacement (like a virtual studio)

✓ Generating stylized videos from images

Fotor and Deep Dream Generator: Image transformation and advanced filters

These tools allow you to apply artistic AI effects and enhance images.

Fotor : Image enhancement and automated retouching

Deep Dream Generator : Surreal Effects and Artistic Transformations

Conclusion: Mastering AI tools for high-performance design

Thanks to advances in AI, graphic design has never been so accessible and fast .

Midjourney is ideal for ultra-detailed artistic illustrations

Canva AI simplifies graphic design for marketing and social media

Other tools like Adobe Firefly and Runway ML allow you to go even further

What if you automated your graphic creations to save time and monetize your skills?

Next chapter: Automate the creation of graphic content and sell your AI services! □

Chapter 3: Freelancing Or Selling Digital Creations

AI has democratized graphic design, allowing anyone to create professional visuals in record time. This revolution opens up lucrative opportunities for freelancers and entrepreneurs who want to sell their digital creations. Whether offering AI design services, selling graphic packages, or automating services, the opportunities are numerous.

3.1. Become a freelance AI graphic designer

Where to sell your services?

Freelancing is one of the best ways to monetize your AI design skills. There are many platforms available to offer your services:

Fiverr : Ideal for offering graphic designs at low prices and gradually moving upmarket

Upwork : Platform for experienced freelancers, with

better-paid assignments

99designs : Specializing in design (logos, branding, web design)

Toptal : For high-level designers seeking premium clients

Tip: Initially, it may be a good idea to offer attractively priced offers to gain positive reviews and build credibility on the platform.

How to stand out despite using AI tools?

With the rise of AI tools, it is crucial to offer real added value to avoid being perceived as a simple user of automatic tools.

Highlight your expertise : Explain how you adapt and customize AI creations

Add a human touch : Work on details and adjust designs according to the client's needs

Create an attractive portfolio : Show before/afters and case studies

Set your prices and attract your first customers

The price of your services depends on your experience, the complexity of the project and market demand . Here is an indicative range:

• Basic AI Logo : 15-50€

• Social media visual pack : €30-100

• AI web design + retouching : €200-1000

Tip: Offer bundle deals to encourage customers to

order multiple creations at once.

3.2. Selling graphic design packs

 Creation and sale of Canva templates on Etsy and Creative Market

Rather than working on demand, a great strategy is to sell ready-made graphic products as downloadable packages.

 Where to sell your creations?

 Etsy : Ideal for creators selling templates and graphic packs

Creative Market : Premium platform for selling graphic assets and templates

 Gumroad : Allows you to sell directly to your audience without high commissions

Examples of popular products:

✓ Canva templates for Instagram posts, stories, YouTube banners

✓ Branding kits with logos, color palettes and typography

✓ Icon packs and illustrations

 Design of icon packs, banners and graphic elements

Graphics packs are in high demand because they save time for entrepreneurs and content creators .

✓ Examples of packs for sale:

✓ Social Media Icon Pack (Instagram, TikTok,

Facebook)

✓ Custom Vector Illustrations for Web and Print

✓ Business card and flyer templates

✓ Automate production and maximize passive sales

✓ Strategies to save time and increase revenue :

Using AI to quickly generate design variations

Create multiple variations of the same pack (different colors, styles)

Optimize product listings with detailed descriptions and SEO keywords

3.3. Offer automated services with AI

Offer express services in AI design

Thanks to tools like Canva AI, Midjourney and Adobe Firefly , it is possible to offer ultra-fast services:

Example of express services :

Logo creation in 24 hours with several variations

Quick design of Instagram or LinkedIn posts

AI Image Retouching and Enhancement

Recommended margin :

·Fast creation = Low price (15-50€)

·In-depth customization = Premium price (€100 and up)

Using AI to deliver visuals in minutes

Leverage tools like :

Looka and Brandmark to create logos in one click

Runway ML to generate animations from images

Canva AI to produce automatically optimized designs

Creation of graphic kits for businesses and influencers

Businesses and content creators need visual consistency . Offer ready-to-use kits that include:

Logos and variants

Visuals for Instagram, YouTube and LinkedIn

Engaging story templates and posts

Example of a premium offer :

A complete "Social Media Branding" kit for €300-500

Conclusion: Building a Profitable Business with AI

Artificial intelligence makes it possible to create a scalable and lucrative business in the field of graphic design.

✓ Freelance : Sell services on Fiverr , Upwork , 99designs

✓ Digital products : Create and sell templates and graphic packs

✓ Automated services : Offer fast and optimized creations with AI

Your goal? Find the model that best matches your expertise and vision.

Next chapter: Automate a profitable AI video business and generate passive income! 🚀

Chapter 4: Optimizing Your Ai Graphic Design Activity

Once you've launched your AI design business, the next step is optimization . This involves speeding up production, improving your brand image, and anticipating market trends. In this chapter, we'll explore how to maximize efficiency, build customer loyalty, and stay ahead of AI design developments .

4.1. Automate and accelerate graphic production

Generate serial visuals with AI

One of the main advantages of AI is its ability to produce images in large quantities while maintaining high quality. To maximize your productivity:

Use specialized AI tools (Midjourney, DALL·E, Stable Diffusion)

Create multiple variations of a design in one order

Take advantage of Batch Processing features

Example of a productive workflow:

1.Defining needs → Identify the types of visuals to produce

2.AI Generation → Use tools like Midjourney to create multiple options

3.Refining and Post-Processing → Enhance images with Photoshop or Canva

4.File Organization → Store and organize your creations for quick reuse

Use scripts and prompts optimized for Midjourney

The effectiveness of Midjourney depends largely on the quality of the prompts used. To improve your results:

Prompt optimization techniques:

✓ Be descriptive and specific (e.g., "Minimalist black and gold logo, luxurious style, transparent background")

✓ Use artistic references (e.g. , "In the style of art deco")

✓ Add Midjourney parameters (-- ar 16:9 for landscape, --v 5 for the latest version)

Advanced Automation:

·Use macros and scripts to generate prompts automatically

·Integrate ChatGPT or other text AIs to refine your descriptions

·Leverage No-Code workflows (e.g. Zapier) to automate production

Create a library of reusable templates

A key time-saving tip is to prepare a collection of reusable graphic templates .

Types of templates to create:

Instagram and Facebook posts

YouTube and LinkedIn banners

Flyers, posters and business cards

By storing these elements in Canva, Photoshop or Figma , you can quickly adapt them to your clients' needs.

4.2. Develop a personal brand and build customer loyalty

Build an attractive online portfolio

A good portfolio is essential for attracting and convincing clients. To make it impactful:

✓ Use a dedicated site (Adobe Portfolio, Behance , Dribbble)

✓ Showcase various projects (branding, illustration, web design)

✓ Add case studies to show your creative process

Tip: Add a before/after to show the impact of your graphical improvements.

Delivering unique designs despite using AI

While AI makes the job easier, it's crucial to personalize each creation to avoid a generic look.

Add your own style : Edit AI images with Photoshop or Illustrator

Play with textures and colors to create a visual

signature

Incorporate handmade elements to give an authentic touch

Example: An AI graphic designer can specialize in a specific style (e.g. "Modern Vintage", "Futuristic Minimalism") to differentiate themselves.

Strategies for building customer loyalty and getting referrals

Winning a customer is good. Keeping them loyal is even better!

Techniques to maintain customer relations:

✓ Offer exceptional service (responsiveness, clear communication)

✓ Create exclusive offers for your regular customers

✓ Offer monthly subscriptions to ensure recurring income

Example: A subscription at €99/month including 5 personalized visuals for a client.

4.3. Explore trends and developments in AI design

Integration of AI in motion design and 3D

AI is no longer limited to static images. It is also infiltrating animation and 3D :

Runway ML : Automatic generation of AI videos and animations

Kaiber AI : Creating artistic videos with AI

Nvidia Canvas : AI-Assisted Painting for 3D

Opportunity to seize: Offer personalized AI animations to brands and influencers.

The rise of Web3 and NFTs for AI creators

Web3 opens new perspectives for AI graphic designers:

Create and sell artistic NFTs on OpenSea and Rarible

Collaborate with metaverse projects (sets, avatars, 3D assets)

Explore smart contracts to protect your creations

Example: An AI graphic designer can sell an NFT collection generated with Midjourney and earn royalties on each resale.

How to anticipate and adapt to market changes?

The design world is evolving rapidly, and continuous learning is essential.

Stay up to date on new AI tools (Firefly, Stable Diffusion XL, DALL·E 3)

Experiment with new features (text -to- video , 3D generators)

Join communities (Midjourney Discord, AI Designer Forums)

Winning strategy: Test new tools before the competition to stay innovative.

Conclusion: Becoming a successful and cutting-edge AI graphic designer

Optimizing your AI graphic design activity means:

✓ Automate and accelerate production using prompts and templates

✓ Develop your personal brand to build customer loyalty

✓ Anticipate trends to stay ahead

Next chapter: Create an AI video business and monetize your content!

Chapter 1: Finding Winning Products With Ai

One of the keys to success in e-commerce and dropshipping is the ability to identify winning products— items that sell well, have little competition, and a good profit margin. Thanks to artificial intelligence, this process is now faster and more accurate than ever.

In this chapter, we will see how to use AI to identify and validate profitable products before selling them.

1.1. Understanding dropshipping and its potential with AI

The principle of dropshipping: selling without stock

Dropshipping is a business model where you sell a product without managing inventory . When a customer buys from your site, you order the item from a supplier (AliExpress , CJ Dropshipping, Zendrop , etc.), who then handles shipping directly.

Advantages of dropshipping:

✓ Low initial investment (no need to buy inventory in advance)

✔ Complete flexibility (you can test multiple products quickly) ✔ Easy scalability

(possibility to automate the business with AI)

Concrete example:

Emma launches a dropshipping store specializing in pet accessories. Using AI tools, she finds a trendy interactive toy and adds it to her catalog. Within weeks, she makes her first sales thanks to automated AI campaigns.

Why AI simplifies product research and management?

AI is revolutionizing dropshipping by making product research and management more efficient .

Big Data Analysis → Detects trends in real time

Description optimization → Automatically writes attractive product sheets

Marketing Automation → Manages Facebook and Google Ads

AI tools that make managing a store easier:

•AutoDS : Automated order and price management

•AdCreative.ai : Automatic creation of visuals and advertisements

•ChatGPT : Generation of optimized product descriptions

Market trends and profitable niches in 2025

Thanks to AI analysis, here are the most promising

niches for the year 2025:

Smart technology and gadgets (smartphone accessories, smartwatches)

Pet products (interactive toys, automatic kibble dispensers)

Eco-responsible and zero waste (reusable bottles, sustainable accessories)

Fitness and well-being (sports equipment, massage and relaxation)

Personalized products (engraved jewelry, custom phone cases)

Tip: Use Google Trends to analyze demand for a product before adding it to your store.

1.2. Using AI tools to identify winning products

Sell The Trend and Niche Scraper: Trend Analysis

These platforms use AI to scan thousands of stores and marketplaces to identify products that are gaining popularity.

How to use them?

1.Filter by niche → Search for products with fast growth

2.Analyze recent sales → Check orders in real time

3.Examine the competition → Choose products with a good demand/competition ratio

Example: On Sell The Trend, an entrepreneur discovers that a neck massager is selling very well in the United States. He decides to add it to his store and launches a targeted advertising campaign.

♂Minea and Dropship Spy : spy on competitors' best sellers

These tools help track the best Facebook, TikTok, and Instagram ads by analyzing:

Most promoted products

The number of interactions (likes, shares, comments)

The content creators who sell them

Concrete use:

1.Look for ads that work

2.Find the product supplier on AliExpress

3.Improve the offer (add a bonus, different design, better description)

Example: An entrepreneur notices on Minea that a facial cleansing brush is a hit on TikTok. He decides to sell an improved version with a heating function to stand out.

Using ChatGPT to generate promising product ideas

Stuck for product ideas? Ask ChatGPT !

Examples of useful prompts:

"Give me 10 ideas for innovative fitness products in 2025"

"What are the trending products for cat owners?"

"Which high-tech accessories have strong sales potential this year?"

Tip: Combine ChatGPT with Google Trends and Sell The Trend to validate the best ideas .

1.3. Validation of a product before selling it

Check demand with Google Trends and Facebook Ads Library

Before selling a product, make sure it has a real demand .

Google Trends : Check if interest in the product is increasing

Facebook Ads Library : Search similar ads to see if they work

Amazon and AliExpress : Analyze reviews and order volume

Example: Want to sell an LED meditation lamp ? If Google Trends shows an increase in searches and several Facebook ads are active, that's a good sign .

Evaluate competition and profit margin

Selling a profitable product also means ensuring that the margin is attractive .

Criteria for a good winning product:

✓ Purchase price on AliExpress : €5 to €15

✓ Recommended retail price: €25 to €50

✓ Low competition and differentiable product

Tip: Use AI to add unique value to an existing product (premium packaging, bonus accessories).

Testing a product with AI advertising campaigns

Before you commit fully to a product, test it with automated AI ads .

Meta Ads + AdCreative.ai : Create attractive ads with AI

TikTok Ads + Pipiads : Analyze which ads work on TikTok

Google Ads + Performance Max : Let AI optimize your ads in real time

Example: A seller tests a portable mini projector by running a Facebook ad for €100. They monitor the results and adjust their strategy based on performance.

Conclusion: Finding the right product with AI, a key asset in dropshipping

✔ AI simplifies product research and management

✔ Analytics tools help identify the best trends

✔ Testing a product before scaling it up ensures profitability

Next chapter: Building an e-commerce store optimized with AI! 🛒

Chapter 2: Creating Automated Stores

A successful online store must be professional, optimized, and automated to maximize sales and minimize time-consuming tasks. Thanks to artificial intelligence, it's possible to create a profitable e-commerce store without technical skills and automate processes like order management, content creation, and customer support.

In this chapter, we will see how to build and manage an automated e-commerce store with AI .

2.1. Building a store without technical skills

Shopify and WooCommerce : the most popular platforms

The two most used solutions for creating an e-commerce store are:

Shopify → Turnkey platform, ideal for beginners

WooCommerce → WordPress extension, perfect for more customization

Quick comparison:

Platform ☐ Advantages ⚠ Disadvantages

Shopify Easy to use, hosting included, many themes   Monthly subscription, transaction fees

WooCommerce 100% customizable, reduced costs, SEO optimized   Requires hosting and a bit more setup

Tip: If you want a quick solution , Shopify is recommended. If you want more control and long-term savings , WooCommerce is a great option.

AI tools to generate product descriptions and images

Creating attractive product listings is essential, but it can be time-consuming and tedious. Fortunately, AI can automate this process.

ChatGPT → Generates conversion-optimized product descriptions

Canva AI & Midjourney → Create professional visuals and product

mockups Remove.bg → Automatically removes background from images

Example: Selling a smartwatch? Use ChatGPT to write an engaging description and Midjourney to create impactful ad images .

Automate tasks with plugins like DSers and Oberlo

Once your store is set up, you need to automatically manage the import and shipping of products .

Essential plugins:

DSers (Shopify) : Connects your store to AliExpress for automatic order fulfillment

Oberlo (Shopify) : Order automation and inventory updates

AliDropship (WooCommerce) : Complete dropshipping automation with AliExpress

Example: Are you selling a fitness bracelet? As soon as a customer orders, DSers automatically places the order with the AliExpress supplier , who ships the product without manual intervention.

2.2. Automatic generation of content for the store

Write attractive product descriptions with ChatGPT

Product descriptions should be persuasive, informative, and SEO-optimized .

Effective prompt for ChatGPT:

"Write an engaging product description for a facial cleansing brush, highlighting its benefits, features, and a call to action."

Example of AI-generated description:

Get radiant skin with our facial cleansing brush! Thanks to its sonic vibrations and ultra-soft bristles, it eliminates impurities and improves the absorption of your skincare products. Easy to use and waterproof, it's your daily beauty ally!

Generate professional images with Midjourney or Canva AI

Creating attractive product visuals is essential to giving your store a professional image.

Midjourney → Generates realistic and high-quality visuals

Canva AI → Quickly design banners and marketing visuals

Mockup AI → Creates realistic scenarios (example: a

personalized cup on a table)

Example: Selling a minimalist wall poster? Use Midjourney to generate stylish mockups in a modern living room .

Creation of an FAQ and AI customer support

A good FAQ reduces the number of customer inquiries and improves the user experience.

ChatGPT & Notion AI → Automatically write a complete FAQ

Tidio AI & ChatBot.com → Install an AI chatbot to answer frequently asked questions

Zendesk AI → Automates customer support

Tip: Add an FAQ section under each product sheet to anticipate customer questions and improve conversions.

2.3. Automate order management and customer service

Setting up an AI chatbot to respond to customers

AI can handle 90% of frequently asked questions without human intervention.

Tidio AI → Answers questions in real time (delivery, refunds, product details)

ManyChat → Manages conversations on Facebook Messenger and Instagram

LiveChat AI → Provides instant assistance with automated responses

Example: A customer asks "How long will it take to receive my order?" → The AI chatbot responds instantly based on the destination and shipping method .

Shipping automation with suppliers like CJ Dropshipping

Fast shipping is a key success factor in e-commerce.

CJ Dropshipping → Offers shorter delivery times than AliExpress

Zendrop → Selects reliable suppliers with optimized lead times

AutoDS → Automates order management and inventory updates

Tip: Offering fast 5-7 day delivery with CJ Dropshipping improves customer satisfaction and reduces refund requests.

Optimizing customer follow-up with personalized AI emails

Sending automated emails helps increase conversion rates and build customer loyalty .

Klaviyo AI & Omnisend → Create automated marketing emails

ChatGPT + Mailchimp → Writing engaging and personalized emails

AfterShip → Order tracking and automatic notifications

Example:

AI-generated cart abandonment email:

"We noticed you left an item in your cart! Good news: we're offering you a 10% discount if you complete your purchase within the next 24 hours. Click here to take advantage!"

Conclusion: Building an automated e-commerce store with AI

✓ Shopify and WooCommerce allow you to create a store without technical skills

✓ AI automatically generates descriptions, images and marketing content

✓ Automation of orders and customer support saves time

Chapter 3: Ai Marketing To Attract Customers

Creating an automated online store is great. But without customers, it can't generate revenue. Fortunately, artificial intelligence is revolutionizing digital marketing , making it effortless to launch effective advertising campaigns, generate engaging content, and optimize email marketing .

3.1. Automated advertising with AI

Creating Facebook Ads campaigns with AdCreative.ai

Paid advertising (Facebook Ads, Instagram Ads,

Google Ads) is a powerful way to generate sales quickly . But creating effective ads takes time and skill.

AI Solution: AdCreative.ai automatically generates highly optimized ad visuals based on your audience and niche.

Benefits:

Rapid creation of attractive and effective

visuals AI-based

analysis and improvement suggestions ⬜ Optimization of colors, texts and call-to-action (CTA)

Example: Do you sell luxury watches? AdCreative.ai can generate multiple ad variations with tailored copy and visuals in seconds .

Generation of optimized advertising texts with Jasper AI

The words used in an advertisement are crucial in capturing attention and encouraging purchase.

AI Solution: Jasper AI Automatically writes persuasive and optimized texts for Facebook Ads, Google Ads and Instagram.

Prompt and efficient:

"Generate eye-catching ad copy for a smartwatch, highlighting its features and a special offer."

AI Text Example:

"New Smartwatch ⬜ Monitor your health and boost

your productivity in style! ▢ 20% off today only! Order now ▢ [Link]"

⚡ Test different versions of ads in just a few clicks

The success of an advertising campaign depends on A/B testing . AI can generate multiple variations in seconds.

Recommended tools:

AdCreative.ai → Generates multiple visuals and advertising texts

Jasper AI → Creates different text variations to test their effectiveness

Smartly.io → Automates Facebook and Instagram ad optimization

Trick : Test at least 3 versions of an ad to see which converts best.

3.2. Content generation for social networks and blogs

Using AI to create viral posts and videos

Social media is essential for attracting customers and strengthening your brand.

AI tools to create viral content:

ChatGPT → Generate ideas and write engaging posts

Synthesia.io → Creates automated videos with AI avatars

Canva AI → Designs visuals optimized for Instagram and TikTok

Example of an AI-generated post:

" 5 tips to boost your productivity with a smartwatch! Discover how it can transform your daily life! #Tech #Productivity [Link]"

Automatically schedule your posts on Instagram and TikTok

Saving time by automating the publication of your posts is crucial for the consistency of your strategy.

AI tools to automate publications:

Buffer & Hootsuite → Schedule and publish your posts automatically

Ocoya AI → Generates and schedules content optimized for social networks

Predis.ai → Create engaging posts and analyze their performance

Trick : Schedule a month of content in advance to be consistent without effort.

Write SEO-optimized articles to attract organic traffic

SEO is a powerful lever for getting free traffic to your store.

AI Tools for SEO:

Surfer SEO → Generates recommendations to optimize SEO

ChatGPT & Jasper AI → Automatically writes optimized blog posts

NeuronWriter → Analyzes top performing keywords

Example of an AI-generated article:

"The 10 Best Smartwatches of 2025: Comparison and Buying Guide" - An SEO-optimized article that attracts potential buyers via Google.

3.3. Email marketing and conversion boosted by AI

Automatic writing of engaging email sequences

Email marketing remains one of the most profitable channels in e-commerce.

AI tools to automate emailing:

Klaviyo AI → Intelligent segmentation and personalized emails

ChatGPT + Mailchimp → Automatic creation of email sequences

Omnisend → Automation of reminders and promotions

Example of an AI-generated email:

Object : " ☐ 10% off your first order!"

Content:

"Welcome to our store! As a thank you, here is a 10% promo code valid for 24 hours. Take advantage now! ☐ [Link]"

Customer Personalization and Segmentation with AI

Good segmentation improves conversions and reduces unsubscriptions.

AI strategies for segmentation:

Klaviyo & HubSpot AI → Identifies potential customers and offers them tailored offers

AI Segment → Classifies customers based on their purchases and preferences

Persado AI → Generates emotionally engaging messages tailored to each audience

Tip: Send different emails to new and returning customers to maximize impact.

Automate reminders and promotional offers

Stop losing customers due to cart abandonment or lack of follow-up.

AI Solutions:

CartStack & Klaviyo → Automatic reminders for abandoned carts

Rebuy AI → Offers personalized product recommendations

AfterShip → Automatically sends order tracking updates

Example of an AI email for abandoned cart:

Object : "Your basket is still waiting for you ⬚ "

Contents:

"You left an item in your cart... and it could be gone soon! Get 10% off if you pick it up now. [Link]"

Conclusion: How AI boosts digital marketing?

✓ Automating advertising with AI allows you to test multiple variations and optimize performance.

✓ Creating AI content for social media and blogs generates organic traffic.

✓ Smart email marketing improves conversion rates and customer retention.

 Next chapter: Conversion optimization with AI to maximize sales!

Chapter 4: Optimizing And Scaling Your Business With Ai

Once your online store is up and running and your marketing is automated, the next step is to optimize and scale your business . With artificial intelligence, you can analyze your performance, expand internationally, and transform your dropshipping business into a true e-commerce brand.

In this chapter, we'll explore how AI can help you scale your business intelligently and efficiently.

4.1. Continuously test and improve performance

Data analysis and optimization with Google Analytics AI

Understanding visitor behavior is crucial to optimizing your store and increasing conversions.

AI Solution: Google Analytics 4 (GA4) incorporates machine learning to automatically identify trends and opportunities for improvement.

Conversion rate analysis and identification of blockages

Automatic segmentation of visitors (new vs. recurring)

AI predictions to anticipate future sales

Example: If GA4 detects that 80% of your visitors abandon their cart on mobile , the AI can recommend optimizing the mobile user experience .

Using tools like Hotjar to understand visitor behavior

Hotjar and Crazy Egg allow you to visualize your visitors' journey through heat maps and session recordings .

Heatmaps : Identify where visitors click the most

Session Recordings : Understand Why People Leave Your Site

AI Surveys : Ask users directly what they would like to improve

Tip: If Hotjar shows that visitors are scrolling without clicking , add a visible purchase button at the top of the page.

Improve conversion rates with AI recommendations

AI tools to boost conversions :

Optimizely AI → Automatically tests different versions of your site

Google Optimize → A/B testing based on user behavior

Personyze → Personalization of the site according to each visitor

Example: If AI detects that a customer views a product multiple times without purchasing, it can offer an exclusive discount in real time to encourage them to purchase.

4.2. Automate expansion into new markets

Automatic translation of the store with DeepL or Weglot

Selling internationally is a great way to increase your sales .

AI tools for translation:

Weglot → Automatically translates and adapts your store into multiple languages

DeepL → Advanced Translation with Contextual Adaptation

Shopify Translate & Adapt → Manages content translation and personalization

Example: With Weglot , your site can be fully translated in 10 minutes , and translations automatically adapt to updates.

Identify the best international niches with ChatGPT

Ask ChatGPT:

"What are the most popular e-commerce trends in Germany, the United States, and Japan?"

Analysis of emerging markets and profitable niches

Identification of products in high demand by country

Suggestions for positioning strategies adapted to local cultures

Tip: Make sure your product is culturally appropriate (e.g., colors have different meanings in different countries!).

Find local suppliers for faster delivery

AI platforms to find local suppliers:

AliExpress & CJ Dropshipping AI → Automatically find suppliers close to your target market

Zendrop → Connects to top suppliers with fast shipping

Faire.com → B2B platform for finding local producers

Example: If you are selling to Europe , find a local supplier to avoid 3 week delivery times from China .

4.3. Transform your dropshipping into an e-

commerce brand

Moving from classic dropshipping to a private label model

Advantages of Private Label:

Higher margins (no need to share with a middleman)

Total control over packaging and quality

Differentiation from competition

Strategy :

1. Identify your best-selling products

2. Find a manufacturer who will accept your logo

3. Optimize your branding and packaging

Platforms for finding suppliers:

Alibaba & Sourcify → Large-scale custom production

Printful & T-Pop → Print on Demand with Custom Branding

Build a loyal audience through an AI newsletter

Email marketing remains one of the best ways to build loyalty and sell more.

AI tools to create engaging emails:

Klaviyo AI & Mailchimp AI → Automatically compose and personalize your emails

Omnisend AI → Analyzes behaviors and sends tailored offers

ChatGPT → Generates newsletters optimized for

engagement

Example:

Object : " ☐ Our BEST-SELLER is back in stock... and you get an exclusive discount!"

Launch a range of personalized products using print on demand

AI enables the delivery of personalized products without inventory.

Print -on- Demand AI Tools :

Printful AI → Generates designs automatically

Gelato & SPOD → Local printing for fast delivery

TeeSpring AI → Creation of personalized clothing and accessories

Example: If you sell t-shirts, offer an option where the customer can add their first name or choose a unique AI-generated design.

Conclusion: How to scale your business using AI?

✓ Optimize your store with Google Analytics and automated A/B testing

✓ Expand internationally with AI translations and local suppliers

✓ Turn your dropshipping into a brand with branding and custom products

PART 7: CREATOR AND SELLER OF ONLINE TRAINING

Chapter 1: Generating Courses And Materials With Ai

Creating and selling online training courses is one of the most profitable digital opportunities today. Thanks to advances in artificial intelligence, designing a structured, interactive, and engaging course is easier and faster than ever.

In this chapter, we will see how to use AI to generate quality training , create educational materials and make learning more interactive.

1.1. Why is selling online training a profitable opportunity?

The growth of the e-learning market

 The e-learning market is experiencing exponential growth.

 Demand for online learning has exploded with digitalization

 Platforms like Udemy, Teachable or Kajabi generate millions every month

 By 2027 , the e-learning market is expected to reach nearly $400 billion

Example: Experts in digital marketing, personal development or finance sell online training courses for more than €500 each , generating impressive passive income.

How does AI simplify training creation?

Previously, creating a training course required weeks of work :

Researching content Structuring the course Creating materials (PDF, videos, quizzes) Editing and publishing

Today, AI automates these tasks!

ChatGPT and Claude AI generate detailed lesson plans

Canva AI and Gamma.app automatically create educational slides

Synthesia AI allows you to generate videos with an AI avatar

The most profitable types of training

The most popular areas are:

Business and digital marketing (Facebook advertising, dropshipping, AI)

Personal development and productivity

Finance and investment (crypto, real estate, stock market)

Tech and programming (Python, No-Code, AI)

Tip: If you are an expert in a field, launch an AI training course in just a few days.

1.2. Using AI to structure and generate a course

Lesson plan generation with ChatGPT

ChatGPT can generate a training plan in seconds.

Prompt: "Generates a detailed plan for a 6-module digital marketing training course."

Detailed structure in modules and lessons

Automatic addition of relevant subchapters

Suggestions for activities and exercises

Example:

If you want to create a course on AI, ChatGPT can suggest the main themes, key concepts and practical cases to include.

Creation of educational materials (PDF, slides, quizzes) with AI

AI tools to generate course materials :

Canva AI → Generates slides and presentations automatically

Gamma.app → Converts text into educational slides

ChatGPT & Notion AI → Create educational PDFs in minutes

Example:

Ask ChatGPT: "Write a detailed PDF explaining the basics of SEO for a training course."

It will generate a structured document ready to be sold or given away.

Automation of content research and writing

Save time with these AI tools:

Perplexity AI → Search for reliable information on a subject

Frase.io & Jasper AI → Automatic writing of educational articles

Quillbot → Rewriting and reformulating content to optimize it

Tip: If you need to write an entire chapter , use Jasper AI to generate detailed, well-structured content.

1.3. Make training interactive and engaging with AI

Generation of examples, exercises and case studies

Use AI to enrich your training with interactive content.

ChatGPT can create practical examples tailored to each topic

Case studies can be generated based on real-life scenarios

Interactive exercises stimulate active learning

Example:

"Give me a practical exercise to learn the basics of Google Ads."

ChatGPT will generate a real-life case with questions to solve.

Creation of quizzes and interactive assessments

AI tools to generate engaging quizzes:

Typeform AI & Kahoot AI → Create interactive quizzes in just a few clicks

Quizlet AI → Educational

Flashcard Generation Google Forms + AI → Test Automation and Fixes

Example:

"Generates a 10-question quiz on SEO basics with detailed answers."

AI produces a quiz ready to be integrated into your training.

Using AI to personalize the learning experience

Personalization = More engagement and retention.

Automatic adaptation of content according to the student's level

AI suggestions to strengthen student weaknesses

Interactive AI tutors to answer questions in real time

Example:

Platforms like Khan Academy AI analyze student performance and suggest personalized content to fill gaps.

Conclusion: AI at the service of online trainers

✓ Create a complete training course in hours using AI

✓ Automate research, writing, and creation of materials

✓ Make your training more engaging with interactive quizzes and exercises

Chapter 2: Recording Training With Ai

Today, it's possible to create professional video training courses without the need for a recording studio or even showing your face. Thanks to artificial intelligence, you can generate realistic avatars, natural voiceovers, and automate editing in just a few clicks.

In this chapter, we will explore the best AI solutions to easily produce quality video training.

2.1. Create a video training without showing your face

Presentation of tools like Synthesia and D-ID

AI avatars allow you to create professional videos without a camera or microphone.

The best tools for generating realistic avatars:

Synthesia – Create videos with animated human avatars

D-ID – Photo animation to speak with a realistic voice

HeyGen – Custom Avatar Generation for Dynamic Presentations

Example:

With Synthesia, you type your text , and the avatar generates a video with a natural appearance and voice .

Generate a realistic avatar to animate the training

Customizing avatars for more authenticity.

Choose an avatar from a library of realistic faces

Customize the avatar's outfit, background and attitude

Adapt expressions and gestures to better captivate your audience

Tip:

Add slides and background images to make your video more attractive.

Optimize tone and gestures to capture attention

AI can make the presentation more dynamic.

Adjust the pace of speech to avoid a monotonous tone

Add natural gestures to reinforce the message

Vary intonations to avoid a robotic effect

Example:

Synthesia allows you to choose between a serious, inspiring or educational tone , depending on your audience.

2.2. Automatic generation of professional voiceovers

Text-to-speech tools like Murf AI and ElevenLabs

No need to record your voice: AI does it for you!

The best tools for a natural voiceover:

Murf AI – Realistic and Adjustable Voices

ElevenLabs – Ultra-smooth text-to-speech

Play.ht – Customizable voices and instant translation

Example:

With Murf AI , you can convert text into realistic narration , with adjustable tone depending on the desired emotion.

Adjust tone, intonation and voice fluency

A monotonous voice can drive your audience away.

Select a narration style that suits your audience

Adjust speed, intonation, and volume

Add natural pauses for better comprehension

Tip:

Experiment with different voices and add light audio

effects to enhance the experience.

Machine translation to sell your training internationally

Reach a global audience with AI.

Translate your voiceovers with DeepL or ChatGPT

Generate voice in multiple languages with ElevenLabs

Add automatic subtitles in multiple languages

Example:

With HeyGen AI , you can translate a complete video into multiple languages without re-recording .

2.3. Video editing and editing made easy with AI

Automate editing with Runway ML or Pictory AI

No more hours spent on editing software!

AI tools allow you to:

Automatically trim unnecessary footage

Add smart transitions and effects

Generate ready-to-publish videos

Recommended tools:

Runway ML – Automated editing with advanced effects

Pictory AI – Generates videos from text

Example:

Runway ML can analyze your rushes and edit a smooth video in minutes .

Add dynamic subtitles and animations

Improve the accessibility and engagement of your videos.

Veed.io & Kapwing → Automatically add subtitles

Descript AI → Automatic generation and correction of dialogues

Fliki AI → Create smooth animations and transitions

Tip:

Add stylish subtitles and dynamic animations to make the video more captivating .

Optimize the format for YouTube, Udemy and other platforms

Adapt your videos to the requirements of the platforms.

YouTube → 16:9 format, duration adapted to the algorithm

Udemy & Teachable → Structured into clear modules

TikTok & Instagram Reels → Short and impactful vertical formats

Example:

With Pictory AI , transform a long video into several short clips optimized for TikTok.

Conclusion: Produce professional video training in record time

✓ Create videos without showing your face thanks to AI avatars

✓ Generate natural and professional voiceovers

✓ Automate editing and adapt your videos to training platforms

Chapter 3: Sales Platforms (Udemy, Teachable , Etc.)

Creating quality training is just the first step to success. Choosing the right platform and implementing an effective marketing strategy are essential to effectively monetizing your knowledge . Thanks to AI, it's now easier than ever to optimize the sales, promotion, and conversion of your online training.

3.1. Choosing the right platform to sell your training

Comparison between Udemy, Teachable , Gumroad and Kajabi

Each platform has its own advantages and disadvantages depending on your strategy:

Platform	Benefits	Disadvantages	Ideal for
Udemy	High visibility, large audience, free		

traffic   Strong competition, course prices often cut short   Beginners looking for an existing audience

Teachable   Complete control over pricing and marketing   Requires generating own trafficCreators wanting an independent business

Gumroad   Simplicity, low cost, direct sales Limited features for learning   Simple sale of training or PDFs

Kajabi All-in-one   solution   (courses,   email marketing, sales funnel)   High monthly cost Entrepreneurs wanting to automate their business

Tip:

If you're just starting out, Udemy can give you an audience. If you want complete control , consider Teachable or Kajabi .

The advantages of hosting on your own platform

Why not create your own training site?

Creating an e-learning platform on WordPress with LearnDash or Thinkific allows you to:

Have total control over prices and promotions

Avoid platform commissions

Build student loyalty via a site and a private community

Example:

Many successful instructors start on Udemy and then migrate to their own platform to maximize their income.

Maximize the visibility and profitability of your courses

Some AI strategies to boost your sales :

Optimize Titles and Descriptions with ChatGPT

Generate promotional mini-videos with Synthesia

Automate SEO with NeuronWriter

Tip:

Udemy works with an internal algorithm : a good title, an optimized description and positive reviews will help you rank better.

3.2. AI marketing strategies to sell your training

Write a persuasive description with ChatGPT

A good description can multiply your sales.

Example of optimized structure generated with ChatGPT:

Powerful hook : "Learn [key skill] in 30 days"

Highlighting the benefits : "Develop [skill] and gain [concrete result]"

Social proof : "Already followed by +5000 students"

Call to action : "Join the training now!"

Tip:

Test multiple versions of descriptions with ChatGPT to see which converts best.

Generate targeted ads with AdCreative.ai

AI can create high-performing ads in minutes.

AdCreative.ai → Automatically generates advertising visuals and texts

Canva Magic Write → Helps Create Engaging Ads

ChatGPT + Meta Ads → Generate persuasive ad scripts

Example:

You can test multiple ad variations and analyze which ones have the best conversion rate .

Automate emails and lead conversion

Emailing remains one of the best ways to sell!

Use ActiveCampaign or Mailchimp AI to send automated sequences

Generate impactful email subjects with ChatGPT

Segment your audience with HubSpot AI for ultra-personalized emails

Tip:

Automated email sequences can increase your sales by 30% by re-engaging hesitant prospects.

3.3. Optimizing your sales funnel with AI

Using AI to Create High-Performance Sales Pages

A good sales page must captivate and convert.

The best AI tools to optimize a sales page :

ClickFunnels AI → Automatic Conversion Funnel Creation

Copy.ai → Generation of persuasive texts for sales pages

Unbounce Smart Copy → Improves visitor conversion

Example:

Unbounce AI can test multiple versions of a page and automatically select the best performing one .

Automation of reminders and promotional offers

Stop losing prospects with smart follow-ups.

ManyChat AI → Chatbots to re-engage visitors

Brevo (ex- Sendinblue) → Automation of personalized promotions

Tidio AI → Sending messages to hesitant visitors

Example:

An AI chatbot can answer frequently asked questions and offer a promo code to encourage purchase .

Analyze performance and improve conversions

AI can detect what's holding you back and suggest solutions.

Google Analytics AI → Customer Journey Analysis and Blocking Points

Heatmaps with Hotjar → Understand where visitors abandon

A/B testing with VWO AI → Test different buttons, texts and offers

Tip:

Use heatmaps to see where visitors are clicking and adjust your page accordingly.

Conclusion: Maximizing your sales with AI

✓ Choose the right platform to sell your training

✓ Use AI to optimize your marketing and automate your emails

✓ Create effective sales pages and test different approaches

Chapter 4: Developing Your Training Business With Ai

Once your first online course is live, the next step is to scale your business and retain your students to maximize your revenue. AI offers incredible opportunities to automate management, engagement, and expansion of your business.

4.1. Create an ecosystem of profitable training

Launch several training courses on complementary

themes

Why limit yourself to just one training course?

An effective strategy is to create a series of interconnected courses , to encourage students to purchase multiple courses.

Example: A digital marketing trainer can offer :

A "Facebook Ads for Beginners" training course

An advanced "Facebook AI Advertising Strategies" training

course A "Marketing Automation with AI" program

Tip:

Use ChatGPT or MindMeister AI to generate profitable and complementary course ideas .

Build an audience through a blog or YouTube channel AI

Free content attracts potential customers to your paid training courses.

How to use AI to produce content quickly?

Writing Blog Posts with Jasper AI to Boost SEO

Generate YouTube videos with Synthesia AI without showing your face

Creating Engaging Posts with ChatGPT & Canva Magic Write

Example:

An SEO-optimized blog with 10 articles on "How to succeed on Udemy" can attract thousands of organic visitors to your courses.

Offer automated coaching services

What if AI could handle some of the coaching for you?

Using AI Chatbots (ManyChat , Tidio , Intercom AI) to answer frequently asked questions

Automated assessment systems to analyze student progress

Personalized coaching sessions with Descript AI (generation of interactive videos)

Example:

An investment coach can use an AI chatbot to offer recommendations tailored to each student's needs.

4.2. Using AI to retain students and maximize revenue

Creation of an AI chatbot to answer students' questions

A chatbot can reduce the number of repetitive questions by up to 70%!

Recommended tools :

Chatfuel → Create an AI chatbot without coding

Intercom AI → Advanced Automated Customer Support

Tidio → AI Chatbot optimized for e-learning

Example:

A chatbot can guide a new student through the course and offer additional resources .

Automation of content updates and additions

AI can continuously generate new educational content.

Recommended tools :

Notion AI → Generation of ideas and course summaries

ElevenLabs → Updated voiceovers with improved intonation

Synthesia → Add new video lessons in just a few clicks

Tip: Regularly

add content to your training courses to increase the perceived value and get more positive reviews .

Build an engaged community around your training

An active community increases retention and cross-selling.

Create a Facebook or Discord group to interact with students

Use Circle.so or Skool for a built-in private community

Generate automatic quizzes and challenges to maintain engagement

Example:

A private group with weekly challenges and exclusive content can increase your training completion rate .

4.3. Internationalization and scalability of its business

Automatically translate your courses to reach a global audience

AI makes it effortless to sell training in multiple languages!

Recommended tools :

DeepL AI → Accurate translation of documents and texts

HeyGen → Automatic translation and lip synchronization on videos

ElevenLabs → Generation of realistic multilingual voice-overs

Example:

A course sold only in French can triple its sales by being available in English and Spanish .

Use AI to adapt training to different skill levels

Personalizing courses helps enhance the learning experience.

Recommended tools :

Knewton Alta AI → Generates tailor-made learning

paths

 LearnDash + AI Plugins → Adjusts content based on student level

ChatGPT → Automatic generation of exercises and adapted corrections

 Example:

 A programming trainer can offer a course for beginners and another for experts , generated automatically.

 Automate the management of registrations and payments

 AI can manage the entire sales cycle, without manual intervention.

Recommended tools :

Zapier AI → Automates student check-in and confirmation emails

Stripe + AI → Intelligent payment and subscription management

 Kajabi AI → Automatic creation of optimized sales funnels

 Example:

A trainer can automate registrations , send course accesses instantly and follow up with inactive students effortlessly.

Conclusion: Moving from a trainer to an

automated training company

✓ Create multiple interconnected courses to increase your revenue

✓ Use AI to automate student engagement and retention

✓ Scalability : translate your courses and automate sales management

PART 8: NO-CODE / LOW-CODE DEVELOPER

Chapter 1: Creating Websites And Applications Without Coding

The rise of No-Code and Low-Code now makes it possible to create websites and mobile applications without any programming skills . These technologies are revolutionizing development and giving entrepreneurs complete autonomy to launch their projects quickly and at a lower cost.

1.1. Understanding No-Code and Low-Code

Difference between No-Code and Low-Code

No-code allows you to create applications without writing a single line of code thanks to visual interfaces and pre-designed blocks.

Low-Code , on the other hand, requires minimal programming to further customize the application.

Example:

An entrepreneur with no technical experience can use Webflow (No-Code) to create a professional website.

A developer looking to speed up their work can use Bubble (Low-Code) to build an application with more flexibility .

Criteria No-Code   Low-Code

Required level Beginner   Intermediate

Personalization Limited High

Examples of tools   Webflow , Adalo , Softr Bubble ,
OutSystems

Why are these technologies revolutionizing web and mobile development?

Cost Savings : No need to pay expensive developers.

Speed : Deploy in hours instead of months.

Accessibility : Allows non-technical people to launch projects without relying on a technical team.

Automation : Easy integration with tools like Zapier and Make to automate tasks.

Example:

An online coach can create a course booking platform without coding using GlideApps or Tilda .

Examples of applications and sites created without coding

E-commerce site with Webflow + Stripe

Task management application with Bubble

Freelance Marketplace with Adalo

Online membership portal with Memberstack

Case Study:

The " Dividend " App Tracker " on Adalo generates several thousand dollars without a line of code !

1.2. No-Code Tools for Building Websites and Applications

Webflow and Framer for creating professional websites

Why use Webflow and Framer ?

Webflow : Ultra-customizable design with an integrated CMS system

Framer : Ideal for animations and a smooth user experience

Example:

A startup can launch its showcase site in a few hours with Webflow and add an SEO-optimized blog system .

Bubble and Adalo for mobile and web applications

Creating a mobile or web application without coding becomes child's play!

Bubble : Ideal for creating a SaaS application (e.g. CRM, marketplace)

Adalo : Generation of mobile applications ready for publication on the App Store and Google Play

Example:

An entrepreneur can create a niche social network

with Bubble by integrating a paid subscription system .

Automation and integrations with Zapier and Make

Connecting multiple tools without coding? It's possible thanks to automation!

Zapier → Connects 5000+ apps effortlessly

Make (ex-Integromat) → More advanced and customizable automation

Example:

Automate sending Stripe invoices for each new order on Webflow using Zapier.

1.3. Developing a No-Code project from A to Z

Find a profitable app idea

An innovative idea is key to success with No-Code.

How to find it?

Analyze Google Trends and Product Hunt

Identify recurring issues on Reddit and Twitter

Use ChatGPT to generate business ideas

Example:

An organization app for freelancers was a hit using Bubble !

Building an intuitive interface with AI

AI makes it easier to create modern and engaging

interfaces.

Useberry → Test user experience before launch

Midjourney & Canva AI → Create attractive visual designs

Uizard → Transform sketches into interactive interfaces without coding

Example:

Automatically generate a UX/UI mockup with Uizard before developing it on Webflow .

Test and improve your project without technical knowledge

A No-Code project must be tested before launch.

UserTesting → Get real-time user feedback

Heap Analytics → Track interactions and improve the experience

Hotjar → Analyze visitor behavior on your site

Example:

Test a Webflow landing page with Hotjar to see where visitors click the most.

Conclusion: Why is No-Code the future of digital?

✓ Creating without coding allows you to test ideas quickly and cheaply

✓ With AI, No-Code becomes even more powerful and

intuitive

✓ No - Code tools allow you to run an entire business without a developer

Chapter 2: Process Automation With Ai

Automation has become essential for entrepreneurs and No-Code project creators. Thanks to AI tools, it is now possible to save time , reduce human errors and optimize the management of repetitive tasks .

2.1. Simplify repetitive tasks with AI automation

Introducing Zapier, Make, and other automation tools

Zapier and Make (formerly Integromat) are two popular tools that allow you to connect applications together and create automated workflows .

•Zapier : Ease of use, integration with over 5000 apps .

•Make : More flexible, with complex and customizable automation options .

•IFTTT (If This Then That) : Ideal for automating simple, personal actions.

Example:

Automate email management : When a form is completed on your Webflow site , send a confirmation email via Gmail using Zapier.

Creating workflows to automate work

Workflows allow you to define sequences of actions between different applications.

Steps to create a workflow with Zapier:

1.Set the trigger : For example, a new order on Stripe .

2.Add an action (Action) : Automatically generate an invoice with QuickBooks .

3.Test and Go Live : Verify that each step works as expected.

Example workflow with Make:

•Trigger : Receiving a form via Typeform .

•Action 1 : Create a customer file on Airtable .

•Action 2 : Send a welcome message via Slack .

Examples of automation in businesses

Modern businesses are using AI to reduce operational costs and gain efficiency.

Business	AI Automation	Result
Marketing Agency	Automate Reports with Google Analytics + Zapier	Gain of 10 hours per week
Online store	Automated Order Tracking with Shopify + Make	Reduction of management errors
SaaS startup	Sending automatic emails to follow up on subscriptions	Increased customer loyalty

2.2. *Automatic content generation and interfaces with AI*

Use ChatGPT to generate dynamic text and responses

ChatGPT is a powerful tool for automatically generating content, whether for articles, video scripts or automatic replies in applications.

Automatic writing : Generate blog articles or newsletters.

Automated Customer Support : Answer frequently asked questions with personalized responses.

Video or Podcast Scripts : Create engaging scripts in seconds.

Example:

Use ChatGPT to automatically write product descriptions on a Shopify store.

Creating interfaces with Framer AI and Builder.io

Framer AI and Builder.io allow you to generate interfaces without coding while offering great flexibility for customization.

•Framer AI : Create interactive web designs with smooth animations .

•Builder.io : Generate and customize pages directly from the visual interface.

Use case:

Create a dynamic sales page using Builder.io to

integrate content generated by ChatGPT.

Integrating AI virtual assistants into your applications

Virtual assistants, powered by AI, have become essential to deliver an interactive and personalized user experience .

Chatbots with GPT-4 to answer customer questions.

Voice assistants integrated into mobile applications.

Dynamic interactions to guide the user through their journey.

Example:

Integrate a support chatbot into a training site to answer students' questions in real time.

2.3. Optimize and manage databases without coding

Using Airtable and Notion as Advanced Databases

Airtable and Notion allow you to create databases without coding, while offering a user-friendly interface and collaboration options.

Airtable : Perfect for managing projects with dynamic cards and links to files.

Concept : Content management and knowledge bases, with multiple integrations .

Example:

Create a customer database that automatically retrieves information via a Typeform form .

Automation of data management with AI

AI tools allow you to automatically sort, analyze, and enrich collected data .

Data enrichment : Use AI APIs to add additional information to customer records.

Predictive analysis : Anticipate customer needs using prediction models.

Automatic update : Synchronize databases between different tools.

Example:

Integrate OpenAI API to automatically generate summaries of reports stored in Airtable .

Use AI APIs to enrich your application

AI APIs enable the transformation of basic applications into intelligent tools.

OpenAI API : Text generation, virtual assistance.

DeepL API : Automatic content translation.

Clarifai API : Image analysis and visual recognition.

Use case:

A mobile application that analyzes receipts via image recognition API and generates expense reports.

CASE STUDY

Case Study 1: Automating Lead Management for a Marketing Agency

Background:

A marketing agency receives dozens of quote requests per day via a form on its website. Manually managing these requests is time-consuming and error-prone.

AI Solution:

1.Automatic lead capture via Typeform .

2.Sending a personalized confirmation email with Zapier.

3.Airtable database .

4. Automatic follow-up via an AI chatbot (ChatGPT) to answer frequently asked questions.

Results :

•Save 10 hours per week in manual management.

•Improved customer responsiveness by 80% .

•Increase conversions through personalized and rapid follow-up .

Case Study 2: Sales Automation for E-Commerce with Shopify

Context:

An online store wants to automate order management and customer tracking.

AI Solution:

1.Triggered via Shopify when an order is placed.

2.Automatically create an invoice with QuickBooks .

3.Sending a personalized confirmation email with Klaviyo .

4.Monthly sales analysis with Power BI to identify trends.

Results :

•reduction in order processing time .

•Improve customer loyalty with automated follow-up emails.

•15% increase in sales by identifying the most in-demand products.

Case Study 3: Automating Customer Service with an AI Chatbot

Background:

A SaaS company receives many recurring questions about using its application.

AI Solution:

1.Integration of a ChatGPT chatbot on the website.

2.Instant answers to frequently asked questions (FAQs).

3.Transfer to human agents if the question is complex.

4.Analysis of interactions to improve the bot.

Results :

•reduction in agents' workload .

•Increased customer satisfaction thanks to quick and relevant responses.

•Collecting data on recurring needs to improve the application.

Case Study 4: Optimizing Human Resource Management

Context:

An SME must manage applications and follow up on interviews, which takes up a lot of recruiters' time.

AI Solution:

1.Automation of CV collection via a Google Forms form .

2.Automatic sorting of applications with a tool like Hiretual .

3.Schedule interviews via Calendly and send automatic emails.

4.Track employee performance with Notion.

Results :

•Save 50% of time in the recruitment process.

•Reduced tracking errors and better interview management.

•Improved recruitment quality by identifying relevant profiles more quickly.

Case Study 5: Content Automation for a Professional Blog

Context:

A content creator wants to publish articles regularly without spending too much time on writing.

AI Solution:

1.Using ChatGPT to generate full articles.

2.Proofreading and improving content with Grammarly and ProWritingAid.

3.Scheduling automatic posts on WordPress via Zapier.

4.Automatic sharing on social networks with Buffer.

Results :

•Productivity increased by 3 times , with 3 articles published per week instead of one.

•Increased engagement through consistent posting.

•Gain visibility on social networks thanks to automated sharing.

In summary: The concrete benefits of automation with AI

✓ Significant time savings on repetitive tasks.

✓ Improved service quality thanks to fast and personalized responses.

✓ Better data management with automated

workflows.

✔ Increased revenue thanks to a smooth and efficient customer experience .

Conclusion: Why is AI automation essential?

✔ Automating repetitive tasks frees up time for high-value tasks . ✔

AI improves the accuracy and responsiveness of services . ✔ Intelligent

data management enables faster strategic decision-making .

Chapter 3: No-Code / Low-Code Monetization Opportunities

3.1. Become a No-Code freelancer and sell your services

•Platforms to find clients (Upwork , Fiverr , Toptal)

• Identify the platforms best suited to your skills.

• Create an optimized profile with project examples.

• Develop a convincing portfolio to attract clients.

•Website and Application Development for Businesses

• Offering customized services for business websites.

• Developing no-code mobile applications to meet the needs of SMEs.

• Offering automated integrations to optimize

business management.

•Pricing and strategies for generating revenue

• Determine an hourly rate or a fixed rate depending on the project. • Offer complete packages including support and maintenance. • Diversify revenue sources with subscriptions and additional services.

3.2. Selling No-Code Templates and Tools

•Webflow , Bubble and Notion templates

• Identify common user needs on each platform.

• Create professional-quality templates with easy customization.

• Use tools like Figma to design aesthetically pleasing and functional interfaces.

•Monetize your automations with Gumroad and Payhip

• Create automated workflows for recurring tasks.

• Sell automation packs for small businesses and content creators.

• Offer bonus how-to guides and tutorials to increase perceived value.

•AI Marketing Strategies to Promote Your Products

• Write persuasive descriptions with ChatGPT.

• Generate promotional visuals and videos with AI (Synthesia, Pictory AI).

• Automate advertising campaigns on Facebook and

Google Ads with AdCreative.ai.

3.3. Create a profitable No-Code startup

·Develop a SaaS without writing a line of code

· Use Bubble or Adalo to design the application.

· Integrate payment services with Stripe or PayPal.

· Create an intuitive user interface with Webflow .

·Finding investors and raising funds

· Prepare a convincing pitch with precise data.

· Present a working MVP to demonstrate the viability of the project.

· Highlight cost reduction through the use of No-Code technologies.

·Evolve towards a hybrid No-Code + traditional development model

· Identify the limits of No-Code and anticipate custom development needs.

· Collaborate with developers to add advanced features.

· Ensure a smooth transition between No-Code and traditional development to guarantee scalability .

Concrete examples:

·Success Story 1: A freelancer who earns over €10,000/month building Webflow websites for startups.

•Success Story 2: An entrepreneur who launched a profitable SaaS with Bubble in less than three months.

•Success Story 3: A Notion template maker who generates passive income with templates sold on Gumroad.

Conclusion:

No-code and low-code offer endless possibilities for generating revenue. Whether selling your services, creating products, or launching a startup, the important thing is to focus on adding value and optimizing your visibility by using automation and AI marketing tools.

Chapter 4: Improving And Evolving In No-Code

4.1. Train quickly and become an expert

•Free and paid resources for learning No-Code

• Online courses: Udemy, Coursera and specialized training.

• Free tutorials on YouTube and dedicated blog articles.

• Community platforms like Makerpad and NoCodeDevs .

•Join No-Code communities and events

• Facebook and Discord groups to connect with

experts.

• Participate in No-Code meetups and webinars.

• Subscribe to newsletters to receive tips and updates.

•Participate in hackathons and AI challenges

• Discover competitions on platforms like Devpost or Hackathon.io.

• Work in a team to acquire new skills.

• Use challenges as a way to strengthen your portfolio.

4.2. Automate and optimize your activity with AI

•AI Tools to Improve Your No-Code Projects

• Use AI to generate content with ChatGPT.

• Automate task management with Zapier and Make.

• Integrate virtual assistants into applications to improve the user experience.

•Use data analytics to optimize performance

• Track performance indicators with Google Analytics or Mixpanel .

• Use AI to analyze user behavior and identify areas for improvement.

• Set up automated dashboards to monitor results in real time.

•Create a No-Code agency and delegate with AI

• Define automated processes for project

management.

• Use AI for lead and customer relationship management.

• Form a hybrid team with No-Code and AI experts.

4.3. The Future of No-Code and How to Benefit from It

•Trends to watch in the field

• The emergence of new, more intuitive and versatile platforms.

• The increasing integration of AI into No-Code tools.

• The rise of No-Code mobile applications.

•Evolution of tools and impact of AI on development

• How No-Code/Low-Code technologies and AI are converging to simplify development.

• Potential risks and strategies to stay competitive.

• The importance of diversifying your skills to stay up to date.

•How to stay up to date and evolve with the market

• Follow specialized blogs and podcasts to monitor new developments.

• Carry out regular technological monitoring to anticipate changes.

• Invest in continuous learning to broaden your expertise.

Conclusion:

No-code is more than just a trend: it's a technological revolution that's transforming the way digital projects are designed and developed. To make the most of this revolution, it's essential to continually learn, optimize processes using AI , and anticipate market developments. By combining no-code with automation and artificial intelligence, entrepreneurs can build ambitious projects without having to master traditional programming.

PART 9: AI COACH (PERSONAL DEVELOPMENT, FITNESS, BUSINESS, ETC.)

Chapter 1: Automating Your Coaching With Ai

1.1. Why is AI revolutionizing coaching?

•Accessibility and democratization of coaching thanks to AI

• AI tools make coaching accessible to a greater number of people.

• Reduction of service costs by automating certain repetitive tasks.

• 24/7 availability to meet client needs without human intervention.

•Save time and automate repetitive tasks

• Automation of appointment scheduling and email reminders.

• Automatic generation of session reports or progress reports.

• Personalized monitoring based on the client's progress and objectives.

•Examples of coaches using AI to maximize their

impact

• Personal development coaches who use chatbots for daily support.

• Fitness coaches who generate personalized programs via AI platforms.

• Business mentors who send automatic recommendations based on performance.

1.2. AI tools to automate your coaching

•AI Chatbots (ChatGPT, Claude AI) to answer customer questions

• Instantly answer frequently asked questions.

• Offer personalized advice based on user responses.

• Offer ongoing support between coaching sessions.

•AI-assisted coaching platforms (Mindvalley , MyCoach AI)

• Integration of virtual assistants to help clients stay motivated.

• Dynamic programs that adapt to each client's progress.

• Automation of action plans with regular follow-ups.

•Email automation and reminders with Zapier and Mailchimp

• Automatic sending of evaluation questionnaires before each session.

• Progress tracking with personalized emails sent

regularly.

• Automation of reminders to encourage session attendance.

1.3. Building an AI-based coaching offering

•Define a profitable niche (personal development, fitness, business, etc.)

• Identify the specific needs of customers in a given area.

• Study the competition to offer a unique and automated offer.

• Promote accessibility and personalization through AI.

•Automate the first steps of coaching (diagnosis, action plan)

• Use smart forms to assess client needs.

• Automatically generate an action plan based on the responses collected.

• Offer continuous monitoring through automated updates.

•Deliver a personalized experience through AI

• Use learning algorithms to adjust recommendations.

• Generate content specific to the client's goals (videos, exercises).

• Create an interactive interface where clients can track their progress in real time.

Conclusion:

AI is transforming coaching by offering personalized, automated, and scalable solutions. Coaches can now maximize their impact while saving time by automating repetitive tasks and leveraging chatbots and AI platforms. By implementing well-defined strategies and leveraging the right tools, it's possible to offer a high-quality, accessible, and innovative coaching service.

Chapter 2: Creating Custom Programs With Ai

2.1. Generate coaching plans tailored to each client

·Use AI to analyze customer needs and goals

• Gather information through interactive questionnaires powered by AI.

• Analyze responses to identify priority objectives and areas for improvement.

• Use tools such as ChatGPT to interpret results and suggest courses of action.

·Automatic creation of personalized programs (sport, mindset, business)

• Generate sports training plans adapted to the client's level and preferences.

• Develop mindset programs to cultivate motivation and perseverance.

• Develop personalized business strategies based on growth objectives.

•Integrate AI recommendations to improve the effectiveness of advice

• Add dynamic suggestions based on progress.

• Automatically readjust programs based on performance and customer feedback.

• Provide targeted recommendations to maximize goal achievement.

2.2. Automate the creation of coaching content

•Generating guides and ebooks with ChatGPT and Jasper AI

• Automatically write support manuals and practical sheets.

• Create motivating ebooks to delve deeper into coaching themes.

• Automate content updates to keep them relevant and current.

•Creating videos and interactive media with Synthesia and Pictory AI

• Produce motivational videos and tutorials in minutes.

• Personalize videos with AI avatars for a more engaging experience.

• Transform text and scripts into captivating visual content.

•Use AI to offer exercises and challenges tailored to customers

• Generate tailor-made sports routines or mindset challenges.

• Integrate daily challenges to strengthen engagement.

• Automate the sending of exercises via email or chatbot.

2.3. Make your coaching more interactive and engaging

•Integrate automated quizzes and assessments

• Create quizzes to assess customer knowledge and progress.

• Analyze results to adjust advice and recommendations.

• Automatically generate personalized performance reports.

•Creating evolving journeys based on client progress

• Adapting coaching steps based on progress.

• Offering new challenges to boost motivation.

• Providing real-time feedback to encourage efforts.

•Dynamic personalization of recommendations thanks to AI

• Analyze data to continuously adjust advice.

• Offer complementary content based on the customer's interests.

• Use AI to identify blocking points and offer targeted solutions.

Conclusion:

Creating personalized programs with AI allows for precise responses to client needs while optimizing preparation time for the coach. Automation tools and content generators can deliver an immersive and engaging experience that evolves based on progress. This makes coaching more relevant, dynamic, and accessible to all.

Chapter 3: Customer Monitoring And Interaction

3.1. Automate progress tracking with AI

•Using Google Sheets and Notion for automatic tracking

• Set up automated tracking tables for each client.

• Use Zapier to synchronize data between platforms.

• Integrate automatic reports generated from progress made.

•Sending personalized reports generated by AI

• Automatically generate weekly or monthly reports

via ChatGPT.

• Integrate progress charts and personalized recommendations.

• Automate sending via email or platforms like Mailchimp.

•Real-time feedback and adjustments through data analysis

• Collect performance data through sensors or connected applications.

• Analyze results to identify areas for improvement.

• Offer personalized adjustments directly via an AI assistant.

3.2. Customer Engagement and Loyalty with AI

•Chatbots and virtual assistants to answer questions 24/7

• Deploy an AI chatbot to instantly answer frequently asked questions.

• Personalize responses based on the customer's profile and progress.

• Use virtual assistants to guide users through their journey.

•Automating personalized reminders and encouragements

• Schedule daily or weekly reminders via SMS or email.

• Send personalized motivational messages to maintain engagement.

• Use tools like Twilio to manage automatic interactions.

•Creating an AI-powered online community

• Set up a community space on Discord or Slack , powered by an AI bot.

• Automate Q&A management and community moderation.

• Organize online events, such as group coaching sessions or webinars.

3.3. Monetize and scale your AI coaching activity

•Sale of subscriptions and premium access to its automated coaching

• Offer monthly or annual subscriptions to access exclusive content.

• Offer a VIP coaching service with advanced AI support.

• Integrate payment options via Stripe or PayPal to facilitate management.

•AI-driven online training and course creation

• Develop interactive training courses with customized modules.

• Use Teachable or Udemy to host and sell training courses.

• Automate access to courses after registration using AI workflows.

•Using social media and AI advertising to attract more customers

• Generate targeted ads with AdCreative.ai to maximize impact.

• Use AI tools to analyze marketing campaign results.

• Set up automated conversion funnels to capture qualified leads.

Conclusion:

Client monitoring and interaction are crucial levers for the success of an AI coach. Automation and AI tools make it possible to maintain a high level of engagement while optimizing processes. Monetization through subscriptions and online courses allows for profitable and sustainable scaling of the business.

Chapter 4: Becoming A Recognized And Profitable Ai Coach

4.1. Building a strong personal brand through AI

•Website Creation and Automated Branding

• Use Webflow or Framer to create a professional website without coding.

- Automate content management with tools like Zapier and Make.

- Generate visuals and logos with AI tools like Canva AI or Looka .

- AI-powered content strategy to position yourself as an expert

- Use ChatGPT or Jasper AI to produce blog posts and newsletters.

- Create video content with Synthesia to share tips and testimonials.

- Schedule social media posts with Buffer or Hootsuite by integrating AI-generated texts.

- Using AI to optimize your SEO and visibility

- Analyze keywords with tools like Semrush or Ahrefs , coupled with AI recommendations.

- Automatically generate descriptions and metadata to improve SEO.

- Optimize advertising campaigns with AdCreative.ai to maximize reach.

4.2. Automate your business to save time and generate passive income

- Setting up an AI sales funnel to attract and convert customers

- Create capture pages and landing pages with Webflow or Leadpages .

- Automate the sending of welcome and follow-up

emails via Mailchimp or SendinBlue .

• Integrate an AI chatbot to guide prospects through the purchasing process.

•Monetizing Coaching Packages and Premium Content

• Sell online courses on Teachable or Podia, with automated access after payment.

• Create personalized coaching packages based on client needs.

• Offer VIP access with advanced AI coaching and live sessions.

•Delegate to AI to focus on the human aspects of coaching

• Automate appointment scheduling with Calendly and Zapier.

• Use an AI virtual assistant to handle administrative tasks.

• Maintain human interaction in one-on-one sessions while letting AI handle follow-ups.

4.3. The future of AI-assisted coaching and how to benefit from it

•Evolving AI Trends in Coaching

• Analyzing the impact of AI avatars for more immersive sessions.

• Exploring the possibilities of virtual reality (VR) coaching with AI.

- Using artificial emotional intelligence to detect clients' state of mind.

•Future opportunities (VR coaching, interactive AI avatars, etc.)

- Offer immersive coaching experiences via VR platforms.

- Use personalized avatars to interact with clients in a more natural way.

- Create personal development paths based on augmented reality.

•Train and stay up to date to evolve with technology

- Take training courses in AI and emerging technologies on Udemy or Coursera.

- Join communities of AI experts to exchange best practices.

- Participate in webinars and conferences to stay informed of the latest innovations.

Conclusion:

To become a recognized and profitable AI coach, it's crucial to build a strong brand while intelligently automating your business. AI tools can save time, attract more clients, and optimize your follow-up. The future of coaching lies in the integration of advanced technologies, such as AI avatars and virtual reality, offering immersive and personalized experiences.

PART 10: AI VIRTUAL ASSISTANT (FREELANCE)

Chapter 1: Making Money As An Ai Virtual Assistant

1.1. Why is virtual assistance a profitable business?

•The Rise of Freelancing

• With the rise of remote work, many businesses are looking for virtual assistants to reduce costs and increase efficiency.

• Platforms like Upwork , Fiverr , and Freelancer make it easy to find freelance work.

• The flexibility of the profession allows you to work for clients all over the world.

•How AI is revolutionizing the virtual assistant profession

• AI tools automate repetitive tasks, freeing up time to focus on high-value missions.

• AI can quickly process large amounts of information and generate personalized responses.

• AI-powered virtual assistants can handle customer communication, scheduling, and even content production.

•Examples of services that can be offered without advanced skills

• Mailbox management with automated and personalized responses.

• Calendar organization and appointment scheduling using tools like Calendly .

• Document and report creation with Notion and Google Docs.

• Text writing and correction with ChatGPT and Jasper AI.

1.2. AI tools to automate support tasks

•Using ChatGPT and Jasper

AI to respond to emails and messages

• Set up response templates for frequently asked questions.

• Automate professional email writing with custom scripts.

• Generate quick and relevant responses for social media and live chats.

•Notion AI and Google Docs to organize and write documents

• Create client databases and track ongoing projects with Notion.

• Automate note-taking during meetings with real-time transcriptions.

• Generate professional minutes and reports in just a few clicks.

•Zapier and Make to automate repetitive tasks

• Connect multiple tools to create automated workflows (e.g., import data from a form to a spreadsheet).

• Set up customer follow-up or invoice sending automations.

• Manage administrative tasks by integrating management tools like Asana or Trello.

1.3. Getting Started as an AI Virtual Assistant

•Define your service offering (email management, planning, content creation)

• Identify your skills and select the services to offer as a priority.

• Create personalized packages to meet the needs of different types of customers.

• Offer flexible formulas: daily, weekly or monthly management.

•Set up an automated workflow to save time

• Automate appointment booking with Calendly and send automatic reminders.

• Centralize customer requests via a collaborative platform like Notion. • Use project management tools to track task progress.

•Create an online presence to attract clients

• Build a simple website with Webflow or WordPress to showcase your services.

• Regularly post content on social media to showcase your expertise. • Use LinkedIn to connect with entrepreneurs and offer your services. • Collect reviews and testimonials to build credibility.

Conclusion:

Becoming an AI virtual assistant is a profitable opportunity for modern freelancers and entrepreneurs. Automation tools and artificial intelligence technologies can streamline administrative tasks and maximize revenue. The key to success lies in creating an attractive service offering and implementing smart workflows to save time and build customer loyalty.

Chapter 2: Automate Tasks (Email, Documents, Etc.)

2.1. Email management and customer service with AI

•Automate Responses with ChatGPT and Chatbot Tools

• Use ChatGPT to generate automated, personalized responses to frequent emails. • Embed intelligent chatbots on websites to offer 24/7 customer support without human intervention. • Set up automated responses for common requests, such as booking appointments or frequently asked questions. • Use tools like Drift, Intercom, or Tidio to integrate AI chatbots and manage customer interactions in real time.

•Sort and organize emails with Gmail AI and Outlook AI

• Use Gmail AI and Outlook AI to automatically sort incoming emails based on importance and urgency. • Set up automatic rules to archive, mark as read, or reply to emails based on specific criteria. • Improve productivity by letting AI prioritize messages, reduce spam, and manage communication flows more efficiently.

•Personalization of responses for effective customer service

• Use intelligent response templates to personalize each response based on the customer and the context.

• Thanks to AI, integrate personalized elements (name, context of the request) for a more human and responsive customer service.

• Implement dynamic responses that adapt to the customer's situation and the available information, thus ensuring a smooth and consistent experience.

2.2. Automated document creation and management

•Using Notion AI and Google Docs to Write Reports

and Presentations

• Use Notion AI to organize information, create summaries, and generate documents from raw notes.

• With Google Docs, use the artificial intelligence tool to automatically write, correct, and reword documents.

• Automate the creation of monthly reports or presentations from pre-existing templates, with dynamic adjustments based on available data.

•Automatic generation of summaries and syntheses

• Use AI to extract key information from long documents and generate clear and concise summaries. • Apply tools like Resoomer or Quillbot to automatically summarize long texts, saving time for analysis and decision-making.

• Generate summaries on meetings, emails or activity reports to facilitate rapid decision-making.

•Automation of proposals and quotes for clients

• Create proposal and quote templates with dynamic fields to automate the personalization of offers.

• Use AI to analyze specific customer needs and generate tailored service proposals automatically. • Integrate tools like PandaDoc or Proposify to automate the creation, management and sending of sales proposals and quotes.

2.3. Agenda management and planning with AI

•Tools like Calendly and Motion AI to organize appointments

• Use Calendly to automate appointment scheduling, integrate directly with client calendars and avoid calendar conflicts.

• Motion AI offers more advanced solutions to optimize the calendar according to the day's priorities and objectives, adjusting appointments according to new tasks and emergencies.

• Automatic scheduling programs based on client preferences, thus avoiding double booking errors and optimizing time.

•Automating Reminders and Task Tracking

• Schedule automatic reminders for important appointments or deadlines via tools like Google Calendar or Microsoft Outlook.

• Create follow-up alerts after meetings or interviews to relaunch actions, or schedule follow-up meetings.

• Integrate automatic notifications to remind clients of pending tasks or actions to be taken, thus increasing the efficiency of the follow-up process.

•Optimize your schedule to maximize your income

• Use AI tools to analyze work patterns and optimize the schedule based on times of highest productivity.

• Smart scheduling programs to maximize productive work time while balancing breaks and periods of creative thinking.

• Automation of administrative and project management tasks to leave more time for revenue-generating tasks.

Conclusion:

Automating email, document, and calendar management using AI frees up time, improves efficiency, and increases productivity. These tools allow professionals to optimize their internal processes, better serve their clients, and focus on more important strategic tasks. AI is becoming a valuable ally for reducing workload while maximizing results.

Chapter 3: Finding Customers And Generating Revenue

3.1. Where and how to find clients as an AI virtual assistant?

•Freelance Platforms (Upwork, Fiverr, Malt)

• Upwork: One of the largest freelance platforms where you can create a detailed profile, apply for jobs, and offer your AI virtual assistance services. By highlighting your automation and AI skills, you will attract clients looking for advanced solutions.

• Fiverr: Ideal for offering specific services (such as email management, automated document creation, etc.). You can create attractive " gigs " that precisely describe the tasks you can automate.

• Malt: A European platform that allows you to find clients in a wide variety of sectors. You can create a profile emphasizing your specialization in AI for virtual assistance.

• Tip: Optimize your profiles on these platforms with keywords related to AI and automation to attract the attention of clients looking for specific and modern services.

•Social Media (LinkedIn, Facebook, Instagram)

• LinkedIn: Create a profile optimized for AI virtual assistants, highlighting your specific skills. You can join freelance or entrepreneur groups to share tips and offer services. Participate in discussions and offer AI solutions.

• Facebook and Instagram: Use these networks to post examples of your work, share client testimonials, and promote your services. Create regular posts or videos explaining how AI can optimize virtual assistance.

• Tip : Participate in forums and Facebook groups dedicated to entrepreneurship and virtual assistance to find potential clients.

•Strategies for landing your first contracts

• Offer free or discounted services at the beginning : Offer your services to your first clients in exchange for testimonials or reviews. This will help you build a reputation and attract future paying clients.

• Create a clear and precise offer : Be specific about

the services you offer. Highlight the use of AI for task automation to differentiate yourself from the competition.

• Networking and referrals : After working with a few clients, ask for referrals and testimonials to increase your credibility.

3.2. Setting your prices and structuring your offers

•Hourly vs. Fixed-Rate Pricing

• Hourly pricing: Ideal for one-off tasks and highly specific services. You can start at competitive rates to attract clients and then gradually increase your rates as you gain experience.

• Fixed-Rate Pricing: Best suited for ongoing projects or automated services over a period of time (e.g., monthly email management, content creation). This may be more attractive to clients who prefer fixed costs.

• Tip: Start your services at a competitive rate, but higher than traditional assistants, because you're offering AI-powered services, which positions you as an expert.

•Offer subscriptions for recurring revenue

• Monthly subscriptions: Create subscription plans for customers who need ongoing email management, scheduling, or content management. This can include regular automatic updates, calendar management, and automated email responses.

• Premium plans: Offer premium plans that include additional services like reporting or data analysis.

•Upselling and add-on services to increase your revenue

• Offer add-on services: You can offer additional services like social media management, document automation, or content creation for existing clients. This allows you to generate more revenue per client.

• Upselling: Once a client is using your core services, offer additional or enhanced services. For example, offer advanced automation of their administrative tasks or proactive management of their customer service with AI chatbots.

3.3. Building a relationship of trust with your customers

•Personalizing Services with AI

• Using AI to Personalize Customer Experience: With artificial intelligence, you can personalize services based on each customer's preferences and needs. Use tools like Notion AI or ChatGPT to adapt your services based on customer feedback.

• Creating Personalized Solutions: Based on customer requests, offer tailor-made automations and AI solutions that meet their specific needs exactly.

•Automate service monitoring and improvement

• Automated outcome tracking: Use analytics tools to

track the performance of automated services. This allows you to suggest improvements or adjustments without manual interaction, while maintaining consistent quality.

• Automated feedback: Collect feedback via automated surveys or post-service evaluations to continue refining your offerings. Use AI to analyze this data and derive concrete actions.

•Using feedback to improve your offering

• Collect customer testimonials: Encourage your customers to share their opinions and testimonials on the platforms where you are present (Fiverr, LinkedIn, etc.). These testimonials will improve your credibility and help you attract new customers.

• Active listening and adjustment: Use customer feedback to identify areas for improvement in your services and adjust your processes. AI can help you automate these adjustments based on customer feedback.

Bottom Line:

Finding clients, setting competitive rates, and building strong relationships are essential elements for success as an AI virtual assistant. By leveraging freelance platforms, social media, and smart upselling and subscription strategies, you can build a profitable business. Integrating AI into your service allows you to offer innovative solutions, save time, and increase efficiency, all while providing superior service to your clients.

Chapter 4: Evolving And Scaling Your Ai Virtual Assistant Business

4.1. Become an expert and specialize

·Differentiate yourself by becoming a specialized AI assistant (HR, e-commerce, finance, etc.)

• Choose a specific niche : By specializing in a particular field like human resources, e-commerce or finance, you can attract a more specific target audience and develop expertise that sets you apart. For example, as a virtual assistant specializing in e-commerce, you could offer services like automating inventory management, answering customer FAQs or creating automated financial reports.

• Become an expert in your field : Specialization not only allows you to differentiate yourself, but also to justify higher rates. Acquire skills specific to your field to offer more precise and tailored solutions.

·Offer premium and tailored services

• Offer more sophisticated services : Develop high-end services that meet complex needs. For example, in the human resources sector, you can offer advanced automation solutions for recruitment, talent management, or employee onboarding processes.

• AI consulting and coaching : In addition to your support services, you can offer consulting or training sessions to help companies integrate AI into their operations. This adds an extra dimension to your services and positions you as an expert.

•How to train and evolve with new AI technologies

• Invest in continuing education : To stay up to date in a constantly evolving field, it is essential to train regularly. Take courses, certifications and attend conferences on artificial intelligence. Platforms like Coursera, Udemy or LinkedIn Learning offer training on AI and its practical applications.

• Follow innovations : Subscribe to blogs, podcasts and newsletters specialized in AI to keep up with the latest trends and technologies that impact your field. This will help you adapt your services to new market expectations.

4.2. Automate your business to generate passive income

•Create a website and an automated sales funnel

• Set up a professional website : Create a clear and simple website that presents your services, your expertise, and your offers. Integrate an automated sales funnel to attract prospects and convert them into customers. Use tools like Shopify , WordPress , or Webflow with automation plugins to simplify this process.

• Use automation tools : Set up tools like Zapier , Mailchimp , or ActiveCampaign to automate marketing, content sending, and lead management processes. This will allow you to generate revenue more independently and efficiently.

•Sell AI Virtual Assistant Templates and Guides

• Create Digital Products : Develop resources you can sell online, such as automated email templates , chatbot scripts , AI task management guides , and more. These products can be used by other AI virtual assistants or small businesses looking to automate their processes.

• Marketplace for Educational Resources : Offering training courses or how-to guides to those interested in becoming AI virtual assistants can also be a source of income. You can offer automated training programs or ebooks on platforms like Udemy , Teachable , or Gumroad .

•Implement subscription services to build customer loyalty

• Subscription services : Create monthly subscription offers for ongoing services, such as email communication management, scheduling, or recurring task management. This ensures regular and predictable revenue.

• Retention and upselling : Offer exclusive benefits to subscribers, such as free consultation hours, personalized services, or automated service updates. This not only allows you to maintain your customer base but also increases the lifetime value of each customer.

4.3. The future of virtual assistance and the opportunities ahead

•The Impact of Advanced AI on the Virtual Assistant Profession

• Evolution of AI Capabilities : Artificial intelligence continues to evolve, and in the near future, it will be able to take on increasingly complex tasks. AI assistants will be able to handle not only simple administrative tasks, but also strategic decisions, customer relationship management, and even creative processes.

• The Augmented Virtual Assistant : Advanced AI could allow virtual assistants to be more proactive, analyzing customer needs and behaviors before they even express them, which will increase efficiency and customer satisfaction.

•Future Opportunities: AI Voice Assistants, Total Service Automation

• AI Voice Assistants : The evolution of voice assistants (like Google Assistant or Alexa) opens new perspectives for automating services via voice. Offering AI voice assistance services becomes an interesting avenue for diversification.

• Complete Service Automation : Companies are looking to reduce their costs and automate all possible tasks. The future of the profession could lie in the complete integration of AI to manage complex operations such as customer relations, project management and even decision-making. By becoming an expert in this field, you will be able to capture these new opportunities.

•Position yourself now to take advantage of the AI revolution

• Stay at the forefront of innovation : By continually educating yourself and integrating new technologies into your services today, you can position yourself as a leader in this field. Early adoption of new AI trends, such as the use of voice-based virtual assistants or still-emerging AI tools, will allow you to stay ahead of the competition.

• Build a solid base of loyal customers : By offering quality services and continuing to evolve with AI technologies, you will be able to retain your customers and ensure sustainable growth in an ever-changing market.

Conclusion:

To evolve and scale your AI virtual assistant business, it's essential to specialize, automate your processes, and position yourself in growing market niches. AI offers unlimited opportunities to develop as an expert, create passive income, and prepare for the future of the profession. By taking a proactive approach and staying up-to-date on the latest technology trends, you can take full advantage of the endless possibilities offered by artificial intelligence in virtual assistance.

CONCLUSION

1. Summary Of The Opportunities Offered By Ai

Artificial intelligence has revolutionized the world of work by allowing anyone to perform profitable jobs without advanced skills . Thanks to AI tools, it is now possible to:

•Create content (articles, videos, visuals, training) with platforms like ChatGPT, Midjourney and Synthesia.

•Automate repetitive tasks (emails, schedule management, customer relations) using tools like Notion AI, Zapier and Google Assistant.

•Launch an online business without technical expertise (dropshipping, coaching, virtual assistance) by leveraging AI tools for product research, website creation and marketing.

Each of the 10 careers presented in this book can be started with little or no experience . AI takes care of the technical aspects and allows you to focus on what matters most: growing your business and generating revenue .

2. How To Choose The Job That Suits You?

If you are unsure about which career to choose, here are some questions to ask yourself:

·Do you like writing? → Become an AI writer or create online courses.

·Do you prefer working on social media? → Become an AI community manager .

·Are you comfortable with visual design? → Try out the AI graphic designer profession .

·Want to sell without stock? → Try AI-assisted dropshipping .

·Do you enjoy helping and supporting others? → Get started in AI coaching or virtual assistance .

·Do you want to automate your business as much as possible? → Experiment with No-Code / Low-Code .

AI gives you the flexibility to try out multiple careers before specializing. The important thing is to start and experiment!

3. Future Prospects And Evolution Of Ai

The AI market is booming and the opportunities are constantly growing . In the coming years, we can expect:

·Even more advanced automation , making these professions even more accessible.

·New , more powerful AI tools capable of producing high-quality content in seconds.

•Unprecedented opportunities , such as advanced voice AI assistants , augmented reality or even personalized real-time AI coaches .

The perfect time to get started and get ahead is now. The sooner you educate yourself and adopt these technologies, the more of a leg up you'll be on the competition.

4. Next Step: Take Action!

Theory is good, but action is better. Here's a simple plan to get you started right away:

1.Choose a profession from those presented in this book.

2.Test an AI tool (example: ChatGPT for writing, Midjourney for creating visuals, Notion AI for organizing your work).

3.Create a first project (an article, a video, an online store, etc.).

4.Experiment and improve with customer feedback and new AI technologies.

5.Generate your first income and develop your business .

The hardest part is getting started. Once you take that first step, you'll realize how accessible and profitable these jobs are thanks to AI .

5. Resources And Tools To Get Started Immediately

To help you take action quickly, here is a list of essential tools and platforms:

AI tools by profession

•AI Editor → ChatGPT, Jasper AI, Copy.ai

•AI community manager → Hootsuite , Buffer, Ocoya AI

•AI Video Creator → Synthesia, Pictory AI, RunwayML

•AI graphic designer → Midjourney, Canva AI, DALL·E

•Dropshipping AI → Shopify, Dropship.io, Sell The Trend

•Training creator → Udemy, Teachable , Kajabi , LearnWorlds

•No-Code Developer → Bubble , Adalo , Make (ex-Integromat)

•AI Coach → MyCoach AI, ChatGPT, Calendly for appointment management

•AI Virtual Assistant → Zapier, Notion AI, Google Assistant

Platforms for finding clients and selling your services

•Freelance → Upwork , Fiverr , Malt, PeoplePerHour

•E-commerce / Dropshipping → Shopify, Etsy, Amazon FBA

•Coaching & Training → Udemy, Teachable , Podia

•Content Monetization → YouTube, Medium, Substack

Training and tutorials to master AI

•Google AI and OpenAI → Free courses on AI and automation

•YouTube → Channels specializing in AI tools and freelancing

•Udemy / Coursera → Automation and No-Code Training

Final Words

Artificial intelligence opens incredible doors for those who know how to harness it. You no longer need advanced technical skills to build a profitable online business.

This book has given you a clear roadmap to get started. Now it's your turn. Make a decision today and begin your adventure in the world of AI!

The future belongs to those who know how to adapt to new technologies. Will you be one of those who get ahead, or will you let this unique opportunity pass you by?

It's your turn!

Need a helping hand getting started? Check out the resources above and take the first step today!